CHOSEN

LAURAINE E. WHITE

LIMITS OF LIABILITY AND DISCLAIMER OF WARRANTY

The author and publisher shall not be liable for your misuse of this material. This book is strictly for informational and educational purposes.

WARNING – DISCLAIMER

The purpose of this book is to educate and entertain. The author and/or publisher do not guarantee that anyone following these techniques, suggestions, tips, ideas, or strategies will become successful. The author and/or publisher shall have neither liability nor responsibility to anyone with respect to any loss or damage caused, or alleged to be caused, directly or indirectly by the information contained in this book.

Chosen
by Lauraine White
Printed in the United States of America.

ISBN: 9781498462495

Copyright © 2016 by Lauraine White

Cover Designed by: Veezie Forbes Design Studio, Atlanta, Georgia
Interior formatting by KUHN Design Group | kuhndesigngroup.com
Photography by: Gerren K.Clark

www.miracle-movement.com

This book is dedicated to my mother, Dell Martin Brown, who passed away in the midst of my finishing this publication. She showed me how to grow old gracefully and that you're never too old to try something new. She passed on a legacy of *love* and *forgiveness* that has shaped who I am. She will forever be missed by all who loved her.

R.I.P. Mama...
(Dell Martin Brown, 1935–2014)

CONTENTS

CONTENTS

INTRODUCTION

It was season six of *American Idol*, and our entire family had been glued to the television every week, as one by one finalists were eliminated from the show. As those that we felt should not have been eliminated were let go from the show, we grew tired of the antics—the best talent would be voted off! It came out of my mouth, "No more idols, please..."

The following day, I thought about my statement with the understanding that there was more to this than met the eye. And as I began writing, I became moved to question my own life choices.

I initially began the endeavor of writing this material as a tool to process my life. As I wrote the things that were crafted by the Holy Spirit, I was in disbelief at the things that I was told to write. So, I later tucked away those early writings although the Spirit of God was telling me to publish this work.

I tucked them away until some of the things mentioned began to happen—true to life. After some things began to happen, I took out my notepads and began to read what I had written in 2006 and 2007. After reading them, I realized that I had an obligation to God to publish this work.

Once I made the decision to publish it, God began to give me new revelation, and He unfolded His plan and purpose to restore the Church and America.

It is not my intention to offend anyone by what I have written. Some of the names have been changed or omitted altogether to protect their identities.

God's plan is to redeem—not condemn. It is my desire only to obey God and deliver this message with accuracy, precision, and integrity—just as it was delivered to me.

I CHOOSE TO FOLLOW

Whoever does not take up their cross
*and **follow** Me is not worthy of Me.*

MATTHEW 10:38

hat do you do when God *interrupts* your life? Do you allow Him to correct your course, or do you run away from Him? Is it even possible to escape God's plan? I was always very fortunate, even when things went wrong, in that somehow they usually ended up right. But 2001–2013 was a pivotal time for me, when God stepped into the chess game of my life and reordered my steps.

With the mortgage debacle and the almost-certain demise of the financial system (i.e., takeover of IndyMac Bank, or Countrywide, sold to Bank of America, the feds taking over Fannie and Freddie, and many banks on the hit list, etc.), I witnessed my world (in 2007 and 2008) as I knew it crumble around me. As a successful mortgage broker, I had many successes and failures, but I do not regret the experience.

I started out as CEO and president of the company and realized that I was in over my head. One night after a long day at the office in 2005, I asked myself some very critical questions that changed the course of my life: Am I the head of this company? Who is *really* the head? I am in business for myself, but am I really in business *by myself*? Upon asking these poignant questions, I realized there is only *one* head. So I switched titles and became president. Who was CEO, you ask? God was! Not long after that night, I received the Holy Spirit in Detroit, Michigan, and my life began to take a new path of discovery. I began a spiritual exploration that has culminated in writing this book.

Yes—God literally *interrupted* my life. He placed me at a crossroads in order for me to make a choice. This book is written out of a lifelong journey to know God's will for my life and to ultimately find the true meaning and purpose for my being here on earth at this time in history.

I had the true fortune of being raised in a loving, Christian home and church family. We were members of the Church of Christ, which believes in very strict forms of worship and a very structured way of life. Instrumental music was forbidden during worship, and women had no role except to teach young children. My father was an elder and a devout Christian that loved God with all of his being, and his number-one assignment was to train his children in the way of the Lord.

I can remember just as if it were yesterday one incident that changed my view of what we believed. There was a couple that came to a revival meeting and wanted to be baptized. As an elder, my father and one of the other elders took this couple out to counsel them. They came back to the congregation and announced that they could not baptize this couple because they had both been married before to other people. They said that in order for them to be baptized, they would have to reconcile with their first spouses! This couple walked away that night totally confused. They could not fathom doing this—and neither could I.

I began to question the very fabric of our beliefs—*silently*. Of course, I would never openly defy our system of beliefs. But a seed of interest was planted in me that day. How could this loving God that I was taught was full of mercy and grace allow this couple to walk away from His salvation? Could His blood not cleanse them of these deeds? Or were there special sins that must be corrected before the blood could cleanse? How far is the reach of salvation? These can be confusing questions for anyone but especially a child. But, because I loved and trusted my father, I never asked him why.

Years passed by, and I became very involved in school activities. My favorite activities were singing and music. Although I have sung all of my life, music became bigger than life in high school. I ate, drank, and lived music. I was the only one out of five children that had the privilege of taking voice lessons (we all had the gift of singing). My parents sacrificed not just their time but also their resources to invest in my musical abilities.

My father was so proud of me. In fact, the day that I was born, my father announced that I would be the next Leontyne Price—a well-known African American soprano in the New York Metropolitan Opera. My father was an avid opera enthusiast and enjoyed attending musical events whenever possible and when finances would allow. We woke up singing and went to bed singing.

My journey of discovery began during my junior year in high school, when my father had a stroke and was in a comatose state for almost a year. At that time, I began to see the true colors of those closest to us. My father was bigger than life for me—I loved him more than *anything*. I could not imagine living my life without him. But now he lay motionless and unable to help me through some very critical years. The amazing thing is that my father had known since he was eighteen years old that he lived with a rather large hole in his heart (also known as a heart murmur). This is the reason that he lived so passionately. God and our family were the most important forces in this world for him, and he lived with a well-defined mission—that all with whom he came into contact would know and love God.

My father lived three years after his initial stroke and died of a heart attack. I now believe that during those three years, God allowed me to see my father's frailties and understand the brevity of life. At the time, I did not realize how God had preserved my father so that my siblings and I would have the benefit of an unusually special upbringing with loving but stern parents who loved God with all of their being. It was important for my foundation to know the love of an earthly father so that today I would be able to cherish my heavenly Father.

During those three years, I also became less dependent on my father and more dependent on myself. I alienated my mother, and it was almost as if I blamed her for my father not being there with us. I felt my life was shattered, and I was alone. I traveled back and forth to school on MARTA (the rapid-transit system in Atlanta, Georgia) instead of getting a ride with my mother. I left home early and returned home late every day. I sang with the college choir and in the ensemble, which meant extremely long days, but I would rather be away from home than face the issues of my circumstances. I hated the thought of coming home to see my father in his state of helplessness. I think it was more unthinkable for me to be so helpless and out of control. I wanted to fix things and make things better, but I couldn't. This was a dangerous place to be. I was now open to demonic forces that I had no idea even existed.

The year after my father's death was excruciatingly painful. Most of what happened during that year I do not remember. I went through the motions of living, but I really wasn't present for any of it, including my marriage to my first husband.

I went to Houston, Texas, for a singles seminar and met my first husband, Glenn. When I got back to Atlanta, he wrote me almost every day, but I could not remember who he was. I was enticed by his letters and his showers of affection toward me.

One month after meeting, Glenn came to visit me and proposed marriage. I turned him down flat. But he just kept pursuing me—writing letters every other day, sending flowers, and making trips to visit me. After six months of this kind of treatment, I fell captive to his advances. On Valentine's Day of the following year, I accepted his proposal, and we were married on June 25, 1983.

It seemed as though immediately the abuse began to happen. In August of 1983, Hurricane Alicia came through Galveston and Houston, and we decided to stay in Houston during the storm. The rain and winds were ferocious, but we made it through the storm. But to my surprise, another storm in the spirit realm was brewing. The enemy had devised a plan to annihilate me. And he was going to use Glenn to do it.

Because we were without power, Glenn strongly suggested that I go and stay with my cousin who lived in Houston on the north end of town. So, I stayed with her for a little more than a week. When I came home, he was not there, but I noticed two wine glasses on the coffee table, and one glass had lipstick on the rim. I went into the bedroom, and the bed was unmade, clothes were everywhere, and there was a pair of panties on the bed that were not mine. I became furious, but I tidied up the living room and kitchen, and I made the bed—but I put the panties in the drawer of our nightstand.

Then he turned around and slapped me so hard that I fell to the floor. He grabbed me by my hair and began to repeatedly beat my head into the floor of our apartment.

After doing all of this, I decided to sit on our balcony for a while until Glenn came home from work so that I could confront him with all that I'd found. As I was sitting on the balcony, our neighbor in the apartment across from ours began waving and smiling at me. She motioned that she would like to come over and talk, so I invited her to come over. When she came over, we made small talk, but I was more interested in making sure I did not miss Glenn driving up. She began saying that she hoped that we would become great friends, since she and "my brother" were in a relationship together. I nearly fell out of my chair! She thought that I was Glenn's *sister*. She saw the shock on my face and was confused. I explained to her that I was not his sister, but his wife, and that if she ever came to my house again, I would seriously hurt her. She was very apologetic as she went back to her apartment. As she was walking down the steps, Glenn drove up and parked in front of our apartment. He acted as if nothing had happened.

When he came into the house, I showed him the glass and the panties, and he said nothing—no explanation—nothing! Then he turned around and slapped me so hard that I fell to the floor. He grabbed me by my hair and began to repeatedly beat my head into the floor of our apartment. The beating continued for what seemed to be forever. And then he left again. Here I was, left alone to try to make sense of this—he was the one who had done me wrong, but he beat me up for it!

The beatings continued with more intensity with each beating, and each time he would come back to apologize for what he had done. But he would always turn things around to blame me for his actions. A few times, I left and stayed with my cousin in Houston, who hated him, but I would not go back home to Atlanta because I would have felt like such a failure. You see, everyone—and I mean everyone—tried to convince me not to marry him. Everyone could see what I could not see. I was not ready for marriage and neither was he. I needed a replacement for my father. I was missing the love of my father, and I had mistaken his affections for the unconditional love that my father had for me. Therefore, I was devastated because my circumstances were worse than when I lost my father. Now I was in a covenant relationship with this man and still was alone. I was alone in a new city where I knew very few people, so I was more alone than ever before.

One night after a pretty severe beating, I called a hotline to see if I could get some help. I was running for my life and needed a place to go other than my cousin's house. I ended up at a women's shelter in Houston. The women that met me there were kind and most of all, understanding. They didn't pressure me—they were interested in my safety and well-being—and they listened. The only thing was that the shelter provided communal living, and I wasn't used to living like that. By communal, I mean women lived in a hall, and there was one bathroom shared by everyone on the floor. For this reason, I didn't stay, but I was introduced to other women that had gone through similar situations to the one I found myself in, and they were trying to put the pieces of their lives back together.

I had some critical and pivotal decisions to make. I decided because I was in a covenant relationship with Glenn, I needed to work things out so that we could live peacefully together. Divorce was out of the question. My religious beliefs would not allow me to divorce him, so I made it my business to stay out of his way. I got to where I preferred him to not be at home. And he got very good at staying away.

I eventually got a job with Gibraltar Savings and Loan in Houston as a teller. Finally, I was free to get out and make some friends.

On my first day at my new job, the FBI showed up to arrest one of the tellers that no longer worked for the company. He had embezzled an undisclosed amount of money from Gibraltar, and his final deed was to write a cashier's check to purchase a Corvette without completing a journal entry to balance the transaction. So needless to say, this was probably the most eventful occurrence during my tenure at Gibraltar.

I loved working at Gibraltar Savings. I made friends with some of our customers, and I enjoyed the daily interaction. It gave me an outlet to pursue my own interests. I had become friends with one particular customer, and we talked almost weekly about what was going on in our lives. But I never shared with her my problems at home.

She shared with me that she had met a nice guy that she had been going out with. She seemed to really like him—but I never put two and two together. But one day, I noticed a piece of paper on our kitchen counter with a phone number written on it. It was written in Glenn's handwriting. I noticed the phone number but couldn't be sure of whose number it was. I brushed it off until one day I had to call her (I will not divulge her name) about her account with us, and it became clear whose number it was that was written on the sheet of paper. At the end of our conversation, I asked her if she knew Glenn R_____. She said that she did, that he was the guy that she had mentioned to me, and that they were dating. I stayed as calm as I could, because I was still at work. I explained to her that Glenn was my husband and that I did not blame her for what happened because I knew she did not know that he was married. But I immediately made the decision to go home—back to Atlanta. I called the airline and made reservations for a one-way trip to Atlanta, Georgia. At that point, I knew I was finished with the marriage. I got on that plane and have never gone back to Houston, even to this day.

About a month later, I found out that I was pregnant. I initially did not want to tell Glenn about the pregnancy, but I knew it was the only right thing to do. His response was for me to have an abortion. He knew that this was not an option for me. I did not and still do not believe in abortion and could not believe that he would be so cold and heartless.

During the months that followed, I did not speak to Glenn at all except to make arrangements to get my car back from Houston. I was blessed to immediately get a job with First Atlanta as a personal banker. Most importantly, I was able to receive maternity benefits from my first day of employment and only had to pay out of pocket for the deductible.

Our son, Glenn Jr., was born on June 4, 1985, and my then-husband decided that he would show up at the hospital a couple of days after our son was born. For some odd reason, I would not name our son right away, although I had chosen a name. Once Glenn arrived at the hospital, he was adamant about naming him Glenn Jr., and because of the abuse that I had endured, I did not object.

After the birth of my son, Glenn began to try to pursue me and wanted to see if I was interested in getting back together. Really, I didn't know what I wanted, but I did feel that it would be best to raise our son with his father and mother if at all possible. It had been a long time since Glenn and I had been together, and he appeared nice and cordial in the beginning.

We were back together roughly a month when he began staying out all night again, and the verbal and physical abuse started up again. He had no sense of what it took to make a marriage work—his parents basically stayed together because of their religious beliefs only. His father would stay away for weeks at a time and would return in the middle of the night and demand that his wife—Glenn's mother—get out of bed and cook him a meal. In later years, his father became more active in church and became a deacon, but he remained an abusive husband.

One night after I fell asleep in the guest bedroom—which is where I began sleeping due to the unbearable abuse—I woke up to use the bathroom. The hall bathroom was right next to his bedroom, and I could hear him talking on the phone. As I was using the bathroom half asleep, I could hear him use language with sexual connotations with whomever it was that was on the phone, and he was making arrangements to meet this person. I came out of the bathroom in a rage. I don't know what came over me—but I couldn't see straight!

He calmly said goodbye to the woman he was talking to on the phone and told her that he would call her back later. After hanging up the phone, he headed for the closet where he kept his baseball bat. At this point I realized I had better take cover immediately. He had such *rage* in his eyes! I ran into the guest bedroom, where our infant son was sleeping, and I locked the door just in time.

He began banging on the door with the baseball bat and cursing and swearing that he was going to kill me—*even if it was the last thing he did!* I began putting things in a bag and trying to come up with a way to escape the apartment. We were on the middle floor, and there was a door from the bedroom leading to the balcony. My only way of survival was to get what little I could carry, wrap my baby in a blanket, and jump from the balcony— and that is exactly what I did.

I didn't know I could move *so* fast. I didn't have time to think—I had to think on my feet. I jumped, dropped, and rolled as I was cupping my baby in my arms. I jumped in my car, and by the time I had started the car, he was outside and realized that I was leaving. He jumped into his car and rammed me from behind. I drove right over the curb in front of me and drove around and out of the parking lot. I had never driven like that in my life—I drove like a maniac! But I was running for my life and the life of my child. I didn't even have time to fasten my son in his car seat—he was lying on the front passenger seat. The amazing thing is that he never slid or moved from his original spot, and he slept the entire time.

I did not see or talk to Glenn for six to seven months after this. At this point, I wanted to bring closure to that chapter of my life, and I decided to talk to an attorney about filing for a divorce. Life as I knew it had taken a real turn—I began living at home with my mom, working full-time, and saving most of my money. It was time that I turned the next corner—*divorce*.

How could someone that started out with so much promise end up like this? I was voted most likely to succeed in high school—but this was not success. I was so ashamed. I dealt with the guilt and shame among my church family. I even dealt with the guilt that I had hurled at myself for making such foolish decisions in my life—mainly to drop out of college and marry at nineteen.

This was the time to pull myself up by my bootstraps. I had lived the last few years just going through the motions, and I was tired. It was obvious that Glenn had moved on with his life, and I felt that it was time for me to move on with mine. But why did I feel so empty inside if I was really ready to move on? There seemed to be a gaping hole in my life with many unanswered questions, and no one had the answers.

I had several friends that tried to give me advice about divorce and what was involved in getting an attorney. After several friends' suggestions, I finally hired an attorney and filed for divorce.

The sheriff served divorce papers to Glenn, and he became enraged. He began calling and threatening me over the phone. He threatened to kill me, and I believed him. He had already tried to kill me the last time that I ever rode in the car with him. As he was driving, he pulled out his gun from the side of the driver's door and pointed it at me. I was fortunate enough to see that we were coming to a red light, and I jumped out.

This time, he sounded more determined than before. He was very belligerent in telling me that he was going to "blow my f***ing brains out." At the time, I was working for Decatur Federal Savings and Loan, and I was very guarded and private about my personal life. There was only one person that I talked to, and we had developed a friendship outside of work. We ate lunch together every day. We had a lot in common—we both were separated from our husbands.

This particular day, Sandra called to see if I was going to lunch, but I had been sick all morning. Glenn had been threatening me all day. His threats had begun to escalate to where this particular morning, he would call and threaten, then I would hang up on him, and he would call right back with even more threats. I ended up being sick and vomiting the entire morning, completely immobilized from the sheer fear of him making good on his threats.

I refused to share this with Sandra, but she obviously heard fear in my voice because she would not just hang up—she began asking a lot of questions. I explained that I had a lot of work that needed to be done and I could not afford to get behind. When the day ended at five p.m., Sandra called again, but this time she wanted to know why Glenn was waiting in the parking lot outside.

At that moment, I began throwing up in a trash can at my desk. I knew he was going to do everything that he'd promised he was going to do. I didn't say a word to Sandra—she knew something wasn't right. She called the police.

Once the police arrived, Glenn was sitting in his car with a shotgun cocked on his dashboard, aiming at the front door of our office building. When he realized that they were after him, he took off out of our parking lot.

Once the police were called, I knew I would not get home in time to pick up my son from daycare, so I called my mother to pick him up. As they turned the corner from the babysitter's house, my mother and sister saw Glenn driving "like a bat out of hell" toward the babysitter's home. He was so enraged that he never saw them pass him.

After putting my son to bed and preparing myself for the next day, I realized that on three separate occasions, Glenn had tried to kill me, but God had blocked each attempt. The first was riding in the car with him; the second was when I was driving on I-285 and he drove in front of me and pointed his gun at me—but the gun would not shoot. The third time, he was going to kill me at my job. With each opportunity, the measures that he took became more intense. But also, God's protection became even more intensified.

In replaying these events, I realized that a force greater than Glenn was at work in these attempts to annihilate me, because the enemy had an opportunity to glance into my future to see the things that God had in store, and he wanted to end God's original plans and purposes for my life. I witnessed God being my Rock, my Shield, and my Strong Tower—He had encamped all around me. But most importantly, He equipped me with the shield of his salvation!

Prior to these events happening, I had no relationship with God—I had religion. I was consumed with what other people thought of me. For the first time in my life, I was amazed that God loved me like this. These events ushered in a whole new world for me and put me on the road to my destiny and the destiny of my children.

In seeing God in action, I was pushed to make a decision—to stay where I was or surrender my life to Him. At that point in my life, I wanted Him, but I also wanted what the world still had to offer. I knew God's Word says that you cannot serve two masters, but I found myself torn in my allegiance.

I eventually divorced my first husband, and the enemy came in a different way. The enemy was determined that no matter what path I chose, he was going to force me to take the low road. I began hanging out with church members that were faithful in their attendance in worship and Bible study but also faithful to club hopping on Friday and Saturday nights.

I got hooked on clubbing all night Friday and Saturday nights and would, with my "self-righteous" self, still get up and go to church on Sunday morning. I would fall asleep during services, and I dressed totally inappropriately. Many times, God tried to send messages, but I wouldn't listen. Unbeknownst to me, I even caused one married couple to have marital issues because of the way that I dressed. The wife called me before the elders of the church to confront me about my relationship with her husband. I had no idea that the way that I was dressing was causing him to fall. Both of them were very dear friends of mine, and we sang in the church choir together. Trust me—I had no intention of causing this type of commotion, but I was so careless in my behavior I could not see what I was doing to those around me and those that I cared about. I was so consumed with numbing my own pain that I couldn't see the effects of my actions.

I was seeking love and acceptance in any way that I could get it. I was easy prey for those that could see my vulnerability, and many took advantage of my easiness. I haphazardly dated on the weekends that I did not have my son with me. I may have been reckless in some of my behavior, but I refused to bring any of those men into my son's life without a real relationship. He was the most important thing to me, and I made sure not to jeopardize his well-being.

After many failed attempts at dating, I made the decision that I would no longer have premarital sex. I realized how empty I was inside. Having meaningless sex with no commitment or relationship had left me completely exhausted and without God. Therefore, I made a conscious decision to save sex for marriage.

The last guy that I dated before my second husband seemed by all indications to be "marriage material"—he was Christian, in med school, and came from a very highly regarded family in the community. We dated for a short period of time when I was faced with the question of sexual intimacy. I would always make sure not to invite him to my apartment and not spend too much time alone with him because I knew that alone time would make it almost impossible to *not* fall prey to my physical needs.

On one particular day, we had a major snowstorm in the Atlanta metropolitan area, and all businesses closed down for a few days. I was at home resting when my doorbell rang, and it was Roderick Ball. He said that he'd spent the night at his sister's house the night before (she lived very close to me at the time), and he just wanted to check on me because of the inclement weather. I hesitated because I had not planned for this type of encounter. My son, Glenn, was spending the night with my brother, and I was alone. This was very dangerous, but I let him in.

I wish I could tell you that I was strong and did not give in to my own sexual desires, but I did give in and I fell. I found that I wasn't as strong as I thought I was.

Within the next month, I dealt with my guilt for giving in and not living up to the standard that I had set for myself, and I made up my mind that I needed to have *the talk* with Roderick about my decision to save myself until remarriage. So I invited Roderick over to have dinner.

After dinner, while sitting across from Roderick, I told him that right before meeting him, I had made a commitment to God that I would not have sex again until I remarried, and that I'd had every intention of keeping that commitment until the day that it snowed and he came over. I told him that we could not have sex anymore unless we felt that our relationship was moving toward marriage. Amazingly, Roderick thought that this was a *good* thing! He was very supportive and said that he would do the same so that we could develop a relationship that was built on friendship.

I was excited because I felt that I had found someone that understood where I was in my relationship with God and wanted to participate on top of everything else. Best of all, I felt that all of the pressure of sex that comes with a new relationship had been addressed and put to bed by bringing it up early in the relationship. Therefore, Roderick and I were free to be friends, without the judgment and pretenses. But silently, I felt there had to be something wrong with him.

Several weeks went by, and during that time, we only saw each other a couple of times but talked over the phone almost daily. We felt that it would be best to limit our time alone together.

One particular night, I fell asleep on the couch in my living room while watching TV, and the phone rang. I answered the phone. It was approximately three a.m., and an unknown woman's voice was on the other end. She introduced herself by name and said that she was Roderick's girlfriend. Then she said that Gail was with her, and she was Roderick's girlfriend as well. She named off about seven or eight women that all claimed to be Roderick's girlfriends, and they were all together in his apartment. They wanted me to join them—their intent was to trash his apartment, tearing and breaking up all of his stuff.

I wanted no part of this. In fact, in that moment, I felt relieved. All this time, I had felt that there was something strange about Roderick going along with not having sex. There *was* something wrong with him—but it wasn't what I thought it was. He wasn't gay—he was exhausted from all of the women that he was involved with.

I talked to the first woman that called me for at least three hours. She had a husband and three sons, yet she was chasing Roderick because of his planned future as a doctor. She risked her future with her husband and her three young sons all for the possibility of what her future could be if Roderick were to marry her.

The amazing thing is that she knew about all the other women all along. She had been privy to his "black book" and had asked him about each name in the book and their importance to him. He obviously was not concerned about her knowing this information because she had her own secrets. She got angry with him because he told her that he was not interested in getting married, so she took it upon herself to sabotage his little network of women.

I was relieved that I did not have my emotions tied and tangled up in this madness because I had been given the opportunity to take the one thing that always destroys a woman's ability to walk away—sexual intimacy—out of the equation. I did not give away the power that I had. I cared about Roderick, but I cared so much more about me. For the first time in a very long time, I felt that I was back in the saddle, driving my life on the right road.

I pitied these women because they didn't see their value—that they were more than this. That they were not defined by what their man did for a living as much as how he treated her…how he validated her…how he promoted her…how he respected her.

I was able to move on because I did not have the emotional scars and attachments to this relationship, giving me leverage to find perspective in moving forward toward my relationship goals.

After this ordeal, I prayed to God with a very specific list of my requirements for the next man in my life. I bore my soul to God about my weaknesses and my shortcomings. My list wasn't very long but precise. It included:

A man that was seeking God.

A man that liked children.

A man that wanted a committed relationship.

After writing this list, I placed the sheet of paper that it was written on in my Bible.

I found solace in my family and friends that were supportive of me and where I was emotionally, especially my mother. She suggested that I get involved in volunteering my time to causes that I believed in to get my mind off of what my life wasn't and concentrate on the needs of others. So, I got involved with the National Council of Negro Women and the campaigns of several local state representatives, including Vernon Jones, who was running for state rep in DeKalb County, Georgia.

I met some real dogs. Most were so awful that it was easy to turn them down. The last guy that I talked to before meeting my second husband was so full of himself that all he talked about was himself. I met him while working on Vernon Jones's campaign.

It was July 1992, and Vernon Jones's campaign workers were having an election party at Vernon's home to watch the election results and to celebrate Vernon's imminent win. For some reason, I could not seem to lose this guy that was so full of himself. He just kept talking and talking. I was trying to get involved in another conversation, so I began a conversation with a couple of other people out on the deck of Vernon's home. The conversation was pretty good and far more interesting than the conversation that I was having with the other guy. One guy was in the military and had had an injury to his eye, which was covered in bandages. He seemed very interested in what I had to say about the issues we were discussing. We seemed to have a lot in common.

Little did I know just how interested he was in me—the conversation ended up evolving into a conversation just between the two of us.

We talked for hours before the final election results came in. He seemed to be someone that I felt would be a great friend, and I was certainly grateful that he helped me get rid of that other guy.

From that day forward, we talked on the phone for at least a couple of hours each day. By the end of the first week, we were making plans to meet at the park on that Sunday. I was afraid to be alone with him because of my promise to God and because I liked him.

How was I going to hold myself if and when he made advances? Was I making too much of all of this? For the first time, I realized just how vulnerable I was when it came to matters of the heart. I wasn't even in a relationship with this guy, and I was already afraid of the possibility of something more happening. I guess my past failures were enough of a deterrent to cause me to be concerned.

So, my plan was to take my son, niece, and nephew with me to the park to be deterrents. We met at the park at five p.m., and the look on his face when he saw me with three children was priceless! He tried to play it off as if it were no big deal, but I could tell that he had not planned for this. But I had to plan my moves with him to make certain that I remained true to my promise—it was not going to just happen.

We successfully got through the evening, and he passed the test. You see, one of the items on my list was that the next man in my life needed to care about children. Check! By all indications, he seemed to be very gentle and caring toward children. So far so good.

As time went by, I found myself falling in love with Michael. One particular evening, Michael called to see what I was doing, and it just happened that Glenn Jr. was with his father for the evening. We didn't talk for long, and about an hour later, my doorbell rang. When I looked out, it was Michael. He didn't tell me he was coming over—he just showed up. I hadn't *planned* for this.

I invited him to come in anyway, and we sat and watched TV for a while, and then he began to make his move. I had mixed emotions—a part of me wanted to stop him, but the other part of me wanted him to continue. You see, I liked the affection and the attention. But how far was too far? Had I already crossed the line by inviting him in when I had no safeguards to keep me in check? Well, I ended the night abruptly making the excuse that I needed to get up early for work the next day. He did not want to go—he had planned to stay. But I could not do it—at least not yet...

The pressure was on, but I wouldn't bring myself to have "the talk" with Michael. I don't know why I didn't, but I was trying in my *own* strength to figure out how to play this game as a woman of God and not as I had in the past, just giving in to my desires.

Every time that we went out together, we would end the night with kissing, and of course I began to become emotionally tied to the relationship. With each time that I was with Michael, I let my guard down little by little—until my defenses were non-existent.

I fell and I fell hard. But check out how God works: when I was tempted, He made a way of escape—I just wouldn't take the escape route given. I gave in to my desires, and afterwards I was so guilt ridden and full of shame—but not enough that I would stop!

God put the brakes on the relationship. Since I wouldn't pull myself back, God intervened. Michael's car broke down on him, and he was having a lot of issues on his job. Therefore, we had limited time together. But eventually, the issues on Michael's job were resolved. Unfortunately, his car was not repairable, which meant that it was more difficult for us to get together. God was trying to give me the opportunity to rethink my actions and make a new plan. To make a new plan, I needed God's direction, and that thought never entered my mind.

About a month and a half after Michael's car broke down, he showed up at my apartment riding his bike. How was I going to turn away a man that rode his bike fifteen miles to see me? The hardest part was that I was now in love with him. This was a dangerous combination—love and passion. Passion drove him to ride his bike to my home, and my love for him was undeniable. So needless to say, I gave in again to my desires.

During this time, I spent less and less time talking to God and more time thinking about Michael and what Michael wanted. It happened so gradually that I really didn't notice the transformation.

Michael became my "morning meditation" instead of God. I talked to Michael first thing in the morning and last thing before going to bed. I had misplaced my devotion from the Creator to the creation. Little did I know that I was setting myself up for a great disappointment because he could never fulfill the deepest longings that *only* God can supply. So many women do the exact same thing—placing a man on such a high pedestal where *only* God should reside.

So much happened during this time—I was laid off from my job, my car was repossessed, and I was in a major car accident near my apartment that slightly disfigured my face while coming home from my new job. So many warnings without my paying attention. God was working hard to get me back on track, but I failed to heed all the warning signs.

The more that happened, the closer we got to each other. After the car accident, Michael took care of me and would pick up my son from school every day. He took me to my doctors' appointments, and the more that he did for me the more I depended on him being there.

After receiving a settlement from the car accident, we ended up buying a house together although we weren't married or engaged. We did quite a few renovations before moving in—refinishing the hardwood floors, painting inside and out, painting kitchen cabinets, and beginning to install a new deck. We went to the house every day to work on different projects around the house.

On one Saturday morning when we were going to tear down the old deck, I woke up, and I was ridden with guilt. I was immobilized—so much so that I stayed at home the entire weekend. Finally, I reached out to God for direction. I could not continue down this road of destruction. I needed to derail this train, and so I did that Sunday evening. I called Michael and told him that I couldn't continue doing what we were doing and not be married to him.

So his solution was that we should get married! This wasn't the way that I wanted to be asked to marry someone, but I accepted his proposal.

The following week, I found out that I was pregnant. At this point, everything changed. All of a sudden, I didn't want to get married. In fact, I wasn't so sure that what I felt for Michael could sustain a marriage for a lifetime. I was determined that I would *never* divorce again.

So I broke it off with him. He immediately flew off the handle. He said that he didn't want his child to grow up on one side of town and he's on the other. But I couldn't see myself marrying anyone—I wasn't ready to remarry. I was so consumed with my own feelings that I never heard the message of his heart about wanting to raise our children together.

I was totally confused about what I wanted or needed to do. How could I have ended up at this place? I needed to get away from everything and everyone so that I could figure things out. So I got in my car with my son, Glenn, and I just drove. I didn't stop for anything—I just needed to be alone with my thoughts.

I had seen so many married couples that married because the woman got pregnant, and most of those relationships were loveless and lifeless. I certainly didn't want that. I wanted what my parents had—a loving, nurturing relationship where they encouraged each other to be their best.

I was afraid. Here I was—one child here with me and another one on the way. My life wasn't supposed to end up this way. And I saw no way out of this difficult situation. I had no other choice—I had to face my issues head-on.

When I got home that night, I had a ton of messages—from Michael mostly and from my brother. Michael had called my brother to express that he was really upset about my breaking up with him and wanted to find out if I had gone to their house. While listening to my brother's message, I realized for the first time that my brother actually liked Michael (this was a first—he never liked any of my boyfriends).

I had a reality check. I needed to fix all of this because I realized that although I couldn't imagine myself remarrying, I also couldn't imagine living my life *without* Michael. I had to accept the fact that the next step in our love was to marry, so I drove to Michael's mother's home because I knew he would be there. I just didn't expect that my brother would be there as well.

I parked, went to the door, and knocked. Michael's mother came to the door, and she was obviously furious with me because she didn't say a word to me. I came in and saw Michael and my brother sitting at the dining-room table. Michael was in tears, and my brother looked so concerned. Michael was a nervous wreck. He thought that I may have done something drastic such as have an abortion. Abortion never crossed my mind—I just needed to collect my thoughts to make sure that I was making the right decisions moving forward.

Michael wasn't hearing anything that I said. He was furious. From the time that I found out that I was pregnant up to that very moment, I had been fully absorbed in my own feelings and what I needed to do for myself. Not one time during this ordeal did I ever think about Michael or what he wanted.

Seeing Michael in this light forced me to view him in a different way. He was raised in a home without his own father, and he had vowed that he would not do the same to his own children. In all of our conversations, I never once really listened to him—never did I listen to his heart as to why he felt the way that he did. After that night, I decided that the right thing to do was to go ahead and get married—as planned.

2

I CHOOSE TO ACCEPT

If you do what is right, will you not be accepted? But
if you do not do what is right, sin is crouching at your
door; it desires to have you, but you must rule over it.

GENESIS 4:7

On August 27, 1993, Michael and I went to the county courthouse to get the marriage license, and while waiting for them to process the paperwork that we had turned in, the clerk returned to announce that the judge was available to marry us if we were interested in doing it that day. We looked at each other with questions in our gaze—*wow*. Is this real? Should we do this *now*? But, we didn't have *rings*—didn't that matter? The clerk said that rings were not necessary for a civil ceremony—another *wow*. Then why should we wait? We were in love, had already purchased a home together, and had a baby on the way.

So, we threw caution to the wind and said yes to meeting with the judge to marry—without family or friends—just us. But I was so nervous. I just knew that it was now or never. I felt that my nerves would probably keep me from saying "I do," although I did not want my child to be born illegitimately.

I was going against everything that I knew to be right—I was pregnant and not married; I was about to marry a guy that was not a member of the Church of Christ; and I had been living a lie by committing fornication. I knew that I was doomed to live eternally in hell without any chance of redemption.

My religious beliefs were so ingrained in me that although where I was at that point in time did not feel like a fate worse than death, I *knew* with every beat of my heart that getting married would correct all of my wrongs and set me on a path to *righteousness*. Or so-called *righteousness*, because religion told me that there was a *righteousness* that I could obtain by what I did or did not do and not based *solely* on what Jesus Christ did for me at the cross.

We got married, and there was no fanfare—no fireworks. We went back to our world as it was before the civil ceremony was performed. Now we had the arduous task of telling our parents that we had gone ahead and married at the courthouse. My mother was disappointed but was grateful that we legitimized our relationship. In her mind, she was relieved that I did the right thing. Michael's mother, on the other hand, being a single parent of an only child, was upset. She had already started planning for our reception and really wanted us to have a wedding—not before a judge but before a minister. She wasn't tied to religion, but she had the expectation that you marry at a church and not the courthouse.

But with time, they all adjusted to the idea of us being married. So, all of the plans changed. Michael's father, who was a chef at what was then known as Stouffer's Pine Isle Resort, reserved the Presidential Suite at the Renaissance Concourse Hotel and arranged for catering of our reception, and we stayed the night afterward in this same suite.

We eventually moved into the home that we purchased prior to getting married and began our lives together. Our daughter was born February 12 of the following year, and when it was time to go back to my doctor for my eight-week checkup, I was pregnant again. I was devastated, and I could tell that Michael was, too. I was so vocal about not wanting another baby, and at times I was downright ugly about it. But we were struggling to make ends meet. Our son was in school but attended after-school care. Our daughter was in daycare, which was very expensive, and to think that we were expecting another baby didn't make for a very happy occasion—just more of a strain on our already depressed finances.

This also put a strain on our relationship. Michael began pulling away gradually—I just didn't notice it at the time. We loved each other, but having one thing after another happen would cause problems for the best of marriages.

But we made the best of the situation, resolving to keep the baby although not knowing how we could afford another baby. About a month later, I had a miscarriage, and while in the hospital, Michael seemed relieved. Although I had been very vocal about not wanting another baby, I found myself distraught and not able to get it together. Initially, I thought that it was just because of the hormones after losing a baby, but weeks went by, and I was still in a real "funk" mood. I needed help. But going through the motions kept me from seeing my state of being.

I was functionally depressed—I went to work
every day because I had to. I did what I needed
to do for my family, but I was empty inside.

I was functionally depressed—I went to work every day because I had to. I did what I needed to do for my family, but I was empty inside. I went to work and went to church, and that was the extent of my activities. And my depression caused a further rift between Michael and me. We would have our blowups and then our make-ups. This kept the relationship interesting but strained.

As a race of people, we have a history of not going to psychiatrists for mental health. I am not really sure why this is the case, but this just was not an option. So, I suffered, and I made everyone around me suffer.

Hurt people hurt people. I didn't realize what pain I was causing everyone because I was so absorbed in my own view of my less-than-stellar life. I had envisioned that I would be so much farther along, specifically financially and in my career, but I had fallen short of my own expectations—let alone what I perceived others expected of me.

On one particular Saturday morning, I woke up more depressed than normal. I was in school to get my real estate license and working full-time, so Saturday morning was precious time to sleep in if possible. But this morning, I woke up early, and after cleaning and getting myself dressed, I sat down on the bed, realizing how drained and burned out I was. I had given to everyone else, but I felt that I had no one to give to me. I was empty. So I picked up my Bible and opened it up. The Scripture I opened the Bible to was Ezekiel 37—the valley of the dry bones. I had never read this Scripture before, but I felt drawn to read it. As I read it the first time, I felt the tears begin to roll down my face. I found my situation of being dry and dead inside connected with God's message of deliverance. Then I heard this in the Spirit: "This is the cure for *your depression.*"

This is what I read:

The Valley of Dry Bones

The hand of the LORD was on me, and He brought me out by the Spirit of the LORD and set me in the middle of a valley; it was full of bones. He led me back and forth among them, and I saw a great many bones on the floor of the valley, bones that were very dry. He asked me, "Son of man, can these bones live?"

I said, "Sovereign LORD, you alone know."

Then He said to me, "Prophesy to these bones and say to them, 'Dry bones, hear the word of the LORD! This is what the Sovereign LORD says to these bones: I will make breath enter you, and you will come to life. I will attach tendons to you and make flesh come upon you and cover you with skin; I will put breath in you, and you will come to life. Then you will know that I am the LORD.'"

So I prophesied as I was commanded. And as I was prophesying, there was a noise, a rattling sound, and the bones came together, bone to bone. I looked, and tendons and flesh appeared on them and skin covered them, but there was no breath in them.

Then He said to me, "Prophesy to the breath; prophesy, son of man, and say to it, 'This is what the Sovereign LORD says: Come, breath, from the four winds and breathe into these slain, that they may live.'" So I prophesied as He commanded me, and breath entered them; they came to life and stood up on their feet—a vast army.

Then He said to me: "Son of man, these bones are the people of Israel. They say, 'Our bones are dried up and our hope is gone; we are cut off.' Therefore prophesy and say to them: 'This is what the Sovereign LORD says: My people, I am going to open your graves and bring you up from them; I will bring you back to the land of Israel. Then you, My people, will know that I am the LORD, when I open your graves and bring you up from them. I will put My Spirit in you and you will live, and I will settle you in your own land. Then you will know that I the LORD have spoken, and I have done it, declares the LORD.'"

I believed the words I heard that said this was the cure for my depression. Every day after this for months, I read this Scripture to gain strength and to find resolve to get up out of the grave of my circumstances—to have the ability to face the challenges ahead of me.

Little did I know these Scriptures would lead me into a wilderness experience before I would realize the full measure of my deliverance from depression.

I completed all of the requirements to become a realtor and went on to affiliate with Metro Brokers/Better Homes and Gardens.

3

I CHOOSE TO SURRENDER—
TWELVE YEARS A SLAVE

Don't you know that when you offer yourselves to someone
as obedient slaves, you are slaves of the one you obey—
whether you are slaves to sin, which leads to death, or
to obedience, which leads to righteousness?

ROMANS 6:16

After this period in our lives, things began to appear to get better. Michael and I were both selling real estate and were doing quite well. Our children were doing well in school, and we were settling into our life together as a family.

Things were going so well that we put our house on the market for sale and found a new home in a very prestigious area of town. We felt like things were really looking up for us. We were scheduled to close both properties on September 11, 2001.

I will never forget—this particular morning, I was watching the news and was in conversation with a client over the phone when I watched as the first plane flew into the south tower of the World Trade Center. My mouth flung open in amazement—I thought, this can't be happening! I hung up from my conversation with my client to make sure that this wasn't made-for-TV action. Then I watched as the second plane flew into the North Tower.

Then I watched as the South Tower plummeted to earth in a pile of dust that appeared to cover all of New York City.

This marked a very pivotal time in our nation's history and in the history of our family. These events caused the delay of closing both the sale and the purchase of our homes for approximately two weeks. But it also began a twelve-year journey that would culminate in a transformation of our Christian walk from one of religion to one of relationship with our Lord and Savior.

We finally closed on both the sale and purchase of our homes and moved into our new house. We were so excited. Things were going well in all areas of our lives, and we were happy to start this new chapter.

Shortly after moving into our new home, I got the bright idea to start a childcare center. I did all of the research and development plans and completed the required training and application for approval for the center. In doing the research, it was determined that our best bet would be to purchase an existing center.

I did everything that I could to prepare my credit to qualify for financing, but every attempt failed. Would all of my dreams be flushed down the drain due to lack of funding? Much to my surprise, my husband rose to the occasion and offered to qualify for funding. His offer took my breath away. In that moment, he became my knight in shining armor. You see, this wasn't his dream—it was mine—and I didn't include him in any of the plans or the successes that were realized through his unselfish offer to help me realize my dream.

While closing on the childcare center, I became involved in writing the business-development plan for Capitol City Bank's mortgage company. I allowed myself to be pulled in three different directions: real estate, the childcare center, and now the mortgage company for the bank.

In all of the chaos of my career conquests that I was busy trying to develop, I lost sight of my marriage and family. My priority moved from my husband and family to developing my career. The main issue was that I stopped taking care of my husband—giving him the time and attention that he needed in order to be the man that we needed him to be.

Most of this time, I didn't realize that I neglected him so. I was just so selfish—there's no other explanation for it. Being consumed with busy work that I had to do was my excuse to continue in such bad behavior.

You see, I loved my husband dearly, but so much had happened. The longer you live with someone, their idiosyncrasies that were once adorable and cute become points of contention. But the bottom line was that I was apparently very insecure in our relationship because of the baggage that I'd brought into it after the train wreck of a marriage that I had come out of.

I would become very belligerent once we were alone regarding how he interacted with other women—not realizing what affect my belligerence had on our relationship. Every encounter dug a deeper hole for our relationship, and over several years of this, we both found ourselves—but mostly my husband—trying to climb out of the hole that had become our marriage.

We both found solace in our work. Out of this practice of escape, we functioned as parents first and husband and wife second, which was so out of God's order! And we both knew we wanted better—we just didn't know how to reorder our lives to establish what was right.

So, instead of putting in the work to make a better marriage, we put our energies into making money. And this pursuit didn't just affect our marriage but our children as well. When we weren't working, we were arguing—about everything.

Slowly, I lost my zeal for the one thing that I loved the most—singing. I usually sing all day—morning, noon, and night. It gives me so much happiness and joy. Many times, singing can pull me out of the worst moods imaginable. All of my life, singing had been the therapy that got me through everything— from a breakup with a boyfriend to the loss of my father. I could always find a song that spoke to my circumstances, and singing that song would give me the encouragement to get back up and try again. But this time, it was as if someone had snatched the music from my heart. I didn't reach for a song to heal the wounds of our relationship during this time because I wallowed in my sorrow rather than grasping for solutions.

We were both damaged goods. He was hurt from his father not being in the home while he was growing up—a precious loss for him because it was the very thing that he longed for. It drove him to do whatever it took to hang in with our marriage because he refused to leave his children the way that he perceived that his father had left him. That was one of the qualities that I admired in him—his resolve to take care of his family.

Now, I was faced with a decision. I was trying to juggle all of the responsibilities that I had created for myself, and all of the balls were in the middle of the air when I realized that I could not juggle everything. I had to make a choice. A decision. After writing the business plan for Capital City Bank's mortgage company, the bank's board decided that they did not want anyone else to run the mortgage division but me.

This caused a huge dilemma for me. Do I continue running the childcare center or run the bank's mortgage company? Well, I had the bright idea that we would have my mother and mother-in-law run the childcare center, and I would go to work for the bank.

During this transition, my oldest brother passed away. He had been a Vietnam veteran and had years of alcohol and drug abuse that crippled his potential. His substance abuse came out of his experiences while a POW in Okinawa, Japan. He was found in the early '80s, and the message of his capture was delivered by our then Congressman Sam Nunn. His death was in direct correlation to his substance abuse because he died of cirrhosis of the liver.

My brother's death was very difficult for me, and I am sure that I made life quite difficult for those around me during this time.

During the summer of 2002, while running the mortgage company, I had to wear all of the hats necessary to get the company to make a profit. In the process, I appeared for news interviews, went to meetings, and joined community-based organizations to get the word out about the company—plus I originated as well as processed mortgage loans.

On one particular day early in October of 2002, I went downstairs in the branch to meet with a client that had come in to refinance her mortgage loan.

The meeting with her started out as most application meetings do, addressing all of the particular questions about the house, the applicant, income, assets, and credit. As I asked the questions of her, a strange look came over her face, and the entire meeting took a turn.

She asked me, "You just lost your brother, didn't you?" My mouth dropped open. I didn't know what to say. She went on to state that my mother was taking my brother's death very hard, and that she had a vision of my mother crying out over his loss—mostly at night. She went on to tell me other things that had recently happened to me, specifically about my relationship with my husband.

She asked me, "Is your husband having an affair?" I responded that I didn't know but I didn't think so. She went on to state that there would be another woman involved with him but that God told her that there would be nothing to the relationship.

She then asked me, "What does $19,000 mean to you?" I told her that I didn't know. That baffled me, but I didn't write it off immediately (I have kept this in my spirit even up to this present time). She told me that some horrible things were going to take place but that God was going to take care of everything and that we would be okay.

By the time that she finished her prophecy, I was in tears. I had only experienced this type of encounter through my grandmother, who had died, and a woman that I had met at a beauty salon.

My grandmother was what you would call a seer. She had the ability to know things in advance of them happening. She knew when any one of her children was pregnant, but she also knew when someone was about to die. One incident that my mother told us about was that my grandmother called her to tell her that she was packing to go to see about her brother because she saw that he was very ill. My mother convinced her to wait until she could get there to take her. Unfortunately, he died two or three days later.

My grandmother hated when fortune tellers would travel around her neighborhood. She didn't like the fact that they were "pimping" their gift. She even saw her own death in advance. She called all of her children, grandchildren, and great-grandchildren to come to Birmingham because she had something that she wanted to share with each one of us personally.

The woman that I encountered at the beauty salon prophesied my miscarriage and the birth of our youngest son. She gave me a word of knowledge speaking to the fact that I had just had a miscarriage. But she spoke to the blessing in my future—that I was already pregnant with a son. She went on to prophesy that we would have multiple businesses—and this stood out in my mind—that my husband and I would grow old together and be wealthy.

Here I was once again faced with a woman prophesying and giving words of knowledge about my recent past and my upcoming future. And I couldn't control my tears. We were sitting in the glassed-in conference room. Everyone could see into the office, but once she began speaking of all the things that had happened to me and all that was going to happen, it was as if the rest of the people on that floor no longer existed.

I was forced to try to keep some composure, and once I came to myself, I realized where I was. You see, I was vice president of the bank and many times in many affairs represented the president of the bank. My reputation was on the line. And I was sure that if I completely lost it in this setting, word would get back to the main office.

In order to keep it all together, I stood up in that moment. As I stood up, so did this woman (whom I do not remember by name). I apologized to her for not being able to finish the application and told her that I would call her later to complete it over the phone.

As she walked out of the bank, I watched her get into her car and drive off. I was in total disbelief and kept asking myself, "What just happened?"

My religious beliefs at the time told me that this wasn't *real*, but my *experience* on that day told me that it most definitely was *real*. How else could it be explained? Her accuracy...her precision...

I ended up calling this woman later, but not to complete the application. I had more questions—questions regarding the encounter that happened between us. I was drawn to her because she was *concerned* about what she saw. Frankly, so was I, and because of that we became friends. She told me that how her gift worked was that once someone was in her spirit, the spirit within her would not leave them without some direction. I was grateful for that but didn't really understand what that meant.

In the months after this encounter, as major events happened between my husband and me, this woman would show up in my office unplanned and unannounced. Each time, she would give more direction and insight as to what was ahead for me.

I came to rely on her spiritual guidance as I began sensing things that were about to happen. She taught me many things about prayer and praying the Word of God through my circumstances—that applying specific Scriptures in certain instances would be like applying salve to an open wound—just the cure that any situation needed.

During this time period, my husband began hanging out at strip clubs. I know now that this was a coping mechanism to get through life without leaving his family. He didn't drink alcoholic beverages and didn't have vices that other people have in order to cope with life's stresses. So, he hung out in the clubs instead of finding solutions for our mess of a life.

During this time, our life together became very hard to endure. Most nights, he didn't come home until two or three o'clock in the morning. As time progressed, it got to where he didn't spend much time at home at all, coming in at all times of the night. Obviously, there was a battle going on within him, and all I could do was pray. His acting out was in direct response to how out of order our home and our marriage were—but I was too close to see it for what it was worth at the time. Again, in my selfishness and self-righteousness, I blamed Michael for turning to the strip club to find passion and compassion, which he should have been able to find at home in abundance. But he didn't. Instead, he received accusations, arguments, and complaining.

Not one time did I as his helper—his rib—ask God what part I played in this mess. If I had done this at the time, God would have given me the answers that I was seeking. But I was busy trying to "be right" instead of doing the right thing.

I did try to reach out to a pastor friend in Macon, Georgia, that I had known for years. I had heard that he was having some personal issues at the church where he was pastor. I used this as an opportunity to ask him questions about what I should do. He listened as I shared with him all that I was going through—only conveying what part Michael was playing in all of this and not what I may have done to assist in it. What he told me I wasn't prepared for. He advised me not to pray for my marriage to be saved. He told me that right then, my husband's soul was more important than saving the marriage. He said what good would it be to save the marriage but his soul to still be lost? He told me to look at him as a brother in Christ and then as my husband. What? Really? I listened to him, but I was so frustrated with this whole situation as I was telling and rehashing the details of our story that I realized how broken I was.

In my brokenness, I started hanging out with friends who were also broken to fill up my time. I was listening to these women in my circle of influence, and they were telling me to leave him. Let him figure it out without me.

I am human. I listened to all of their advice and was headed for divorce. I made an appointment with a divorce attorney. At the appointment, I was given my options in filing for divorce, but no one discussed the option of not getting a divorce. In the middle of the interview process, I began to feel sick to my stomach—probably a direct result of the idea of *what* I was really doing. We both had vowed never to leave each other—that we would make it through thick and thin. But *thick* had become too *thin* to save.

Was it this easy to throw away everything that we had? I was an emotional wreck. I couldn't imagine living my life without him. While in the bathroom stall at the attorney's office, it was as if I had a vision of our children, specifically our daughter, growing up without their father. It was not very pleasant. It was so repulsive that I changed my mind about getting a divorce. I went back into the attorney's office and explained that I'd had a change of heart and decided to wait on filing for divorce.

That night, when my husband came home, he didn't look the same anymore. There was something very evil about his persona. When I looked at him, I saw a demon. Was this possible? Things were moving very quickly. I didn't know all that was happening with him, but he was hanging out with a new set of friends. He bought a new Mercedes-Benz CLK convertible and was dressing very differently. It gave me concern—so much so that I lived almost daily with anxiety about what I was seeing.

That Friday after my meeting with the attorney, I was at our church's Prayer Warriors meeting. As a part of our regular times for praying, we would spend the first fifteen to thirty minutes in study on the effect of our prayers. This particular night, after the Bible discussion was over, I raised my hand to ask the question, "Can a Christian be demon possessed?" The looks that I received were cold and condescending, as if to ask, "How dare you ask such a stupid question?" But I asked the same question again to let them know that I was expecting an answer. I wasn't being disrespectful, but I was in the midst of turmoil in my home, and I needed the relief that they talked about because my prayers alone were not producing the results that they ought to based on their teaching.

The answer that I received was not hopeful because it did not reflect my experience. They told me that demons could not possess a Christian because the blood of Jesus purchased us. They went on to *pontificate* that the only thing that demons could do to a Christian was oppress them.

Needless to say, I left that meeting confused and hopeless. If someone asked a question like that, shouldn't someone on the leadership team pull them to the side to find out what they were battling? And just because I was considered a part of leadership, should there be reluctance in approaching the subject in a private setting after prayer was over? None of this ever happened.

Beyond all of these obvious questions, what they were telling me didn't line up with what I was experiencing. My husband was clearly a Christian, purchased by the blood of Jesus, but I physically saw a demon when I looked at him. How do you explain what I was experiencing? I felt that I had no one to help me...

But God—God always sent this woman I encountered at the bank to help guide me through my spiritual birthing process. She taught me how to pray, intercede, and interpret what was happening in the Spirit and then intercept the plans of the enemy during these very pivotal moments in time. She took me to the Scripture that references the building of the temple of the Lord, 1 Kings 6. After reading the Scripture together, she explained the comparison between the physical temple and the temple that is in each of us, both of which are dwelling places for God. She explained that the physical temple has an outer court, an inner court, and the holy of holies. The outer court is our flesh; the inner court is where our soul resides; and the holy of holies is our spirit. In the outer court (flesh) and the inner court (soul), demons *can* possess Christians and oftentimes do by way of entry points. These entry points are the eyes— what you see; ears—what you hear and listen to; mouth—what comes out of it; and nose—what you smell. Without guarding these entry points, demons will take possession because our practice in whatever area has given them a right to enter. The holy of holies cannot be penetrated by demons because this is where the spirit dwells *only*, and God's Spirit has ownership of our spirits.

She went on to explain how demons were able to possess my husband. She said that, in essence, because he regularly went to strip clubs, allowing nude women to dance in his lap, he gave entry to demon possession, and obviously, demons had used all of the entry points to enter him.

This time, her concern grew so much that she told me that it was time for us to fast. The fast was going to be for forty days. Whoa! I didn't know anything about fasting. She then asked me if I knew what it meant to pray in the Spirit. There again, I'd never heard of praying in the Spirit. She instructed me on how to fast—nothing to eat or drink except for water. She said to refrain from watching TV for more than one hour per day but that praying was the essential part to the process. This was not just about praying but about *what* to pray—being specific.

She gave me tactical strategies for spiritual warfare. She impressed upon me the importance of my role in praying for my husband—that as his "rib," which is the covering for the most vital organs in the body, I had the responsibility spiritually to cover him in prayer. She explained that I shouldn't have other people praying for my husband—that only I should do that. If others were to pray, they needed to pray for me to have strength as I went into war for him. She went on to state that she and I would pray together every morning, noon, and night before I went to bed. She would pray in tongues, and I would pray prayers that I would write down. I prayed these prayers during our time together as well as at the top of every hour of every day during the forty days. The prayers that I wrote down to pray every day were:

1. I pray in the name of Jesus that You, Lord God, would lift and remove the veil over my husband, Michael.

2. I pray in the name of Jesus for the Holy Spirit to not just indwell but also hover over him and protect him.

3. I pray in the name of Jesus for godly and righteous people to be in his pathway each and every day.

4. I pray in the name of Jesus that You, Lord God, would cast down anything that would exalt itself against the knowledge of Jesus Christ—specifically lust, pornography, adultery, pride, rebellion, materialism, and fear.

5. I pray in the mighty name of Jesus for You, Lord God, to take down all strongholds and generational curses—thought patterns, opinions on religion, lust, pornography, adultery, pride, rebellion, materialism, and fear.

6. I pray, dear Father in heaven, that You will bind Satan from taking my husband, Michael, captive, loose in him Your spiritual DNA, and create in him an atmosphere for You, Lord God, to dwell. I pray that You, O Lord, will bind all wicked thoughts and lies Satan

would try to place in Michael's mind and loose in their place Your Spirit that brings love, joy, peace, longsuffering, understanding, and generosity.

7. I pray in the name of Jesus that You place the armor of God on him.

8. I pray in the name of Jesus that You, Lord God, will cast out all spirits of perversion, to include: lust, pornography, adultery, pride, rebellion, materialism, and fear.

9. I pray in the matchless name of Jesus that my husband, Michael, will finally submit and surrender his life to Jesus Christ and become obedient to God's will—no matter what. Amen!

Those forty days of fasting and praying produced some hell-raising circumstances. I had no idea that fasting would cause so much chaos in the spirit realm. Naïve me...I thought fasting would produce an easy fix to our problems. It did just the opposite. Things between us got far worse. It obviously upset the demonic kingdom to know that I would gain power by knowing who I am in the Spirit through my experience in fasting and praying.

The fast did open the door to supernatural occurrences that set our lives on an irreversible course to finding our place in God. My mother shared a dream that she had during this time where she could see Michael and me with our children in our home. While sitting in our home, a boulder fell out of heaven, hitting our house. The amazing part of her dream was what happened next. She saw angels ascending and descending from heaven, carrying the pieces of the shattered boulder out of our house. As the angels entered our house, it would light up brightly as they worked to put our home back together. She did not share this dream with me until several years later as she saw God unfold this dream before her.

Also, toward the end of this fast—there were seven days left in the fast—a woman that was visiting Cornerstone Church during our weekly worship service stood up after worship was over to make comments. She said that God told her to drive down Bethsaida Road and then to drive into the parking lot of Cornerstone Church. Once inside, God told her that she was there to deliver a message to someone regarding what they were going through. She said that she didn't know who it was that God wanted her to deliver this message to, but that whoever it was had been through hell. She said that God wanted her to deliver the message that—whoever it was—they were making progress in the Spirit and not to give up just because it looked too difficult and there was no clear end in sight. She prophesied that *pushing* was the next step. She said that this was a *spiritual birthing* and *it* would come forth like having a baby.

I nearly passed out as I listened to this woman, because I knew the message was for me. Everything during this forty-day fast had culminated in this point of *birthing* out our next chapter.

All that week, I could barely walk. I walked wide-legged due to extreme pain in my upper thighs and lower back. I experienced excruciating pains in my lower abdomen every day of that week as if I were *pregnant* and ready *to deliver.*

At the end of that week, on Friday night, my husband wouldn't come home. He called me, sounding very strange. He was talking about how he felt that his life was so worthless and that he had messed up everything. I tried to reassure him that whatever he had done could be corrected and that I forgave him. But he continued in this guilt-ridden talk, and it was very concerning to me. So I asked him where he was, but he wouldn't tell me. My concern was his state of mind. He didn't talk as if he had much confidence in his ability to get past whatever circumstances had arisen and in the fact that we loved him. What was most concerning to me was that he didn't believe that God loved or could *forgive* him.

I asked him to come home—whatever it was that he was dealing with, we could get through it together. He finally came home early Saturday morning about six or seven a.m. He came into our bedroom and slumped down on the side of the bed, and as I got up out of the bed, he moved to the seating at the bay window.

As we talked, his tears began to roll down his face, and he slumped further, with his head almost between his knees. As I watched him appearing to fall apart, I *saw* the demonic spirits leave him, moving toward and out the window.

Months before while in prayer, I had asked God to allow me to see the demons leave his body, and here I was in this moment experiencing this transformation take place. I didn't know what to do because as the demons left his body, they left him with a feeling of defeat and the guilt of his circumstances.

> As I watched him appearing to fall apart,
> I *saw* the demonic spirits leave him, moving
> toward and out the window.

From this moment on, things moved very quickly. Because of his state of mind and my heightened sense of self-righteousness because of what I had just witnessed, we argued even more than normal. One particular evening after dinner, we were engulfed in a heated argument in the kitchen. As I was turning around to walk out of the room, he grabbed a Pyrex dish and slammed it on the counter, smashing the dish to pieces.

As the dish shattered, a piece of the dish lodged itself into the eyebrow of our youngest son. Panic immediately came over both of us. Oh my God! There was no time to place blame and no time to think. We had to move quickly. My husband picked up our son, and we both got in our SUV and headed speedily to the hospital.

On the ride to the hospital, Michael was so distraught and again full of guilt and shame. The amazing thing is that our son never once bled at the spot where the piece lodged in his head, and he never once cried.

Once at DeKalb Medical, the staff moved very quickly to provide the necessary medical treatment that our son needed. They were also concerned as to how this incident happened, so they began an investigation.

One of the nurses helping our son called for a pastor that worked as clergy for the hospital. This pastor met my husband and me out in the hallway to discuss the incident, and my husband seemed to connect with him. This pastor explained his own difficult circumstances and that he had been a pastor in Ohio but was let go because he and his wife had divorced due to *her* infidelity—he was judged because of the actions of others. Finding himself out of a job, he decided to move to Georgia in order to start his life over. After many interviews, he ended up being offered the job of clergy for the hospital—just a month before this incident. This pastor offered for my husband to go with him to his office to talk further, and I was suddenly left alone.

Once alone, an investigator met me in the hallway of the hospital to discuss what had happened to cause this accident. After telling the story of what had transpired, she explained the process of the investigation—that a report would be generated, DFCS would initiate home visits, a caseworker would meet with my husband and me individually and also with our son, and then a determination would be made as to recommendations for remedy.

In looking back, I can see the hand of God working from the moment that our son—who was clinging on to me while my husband and I argued—innocently stood by when the Pyrex dish shattered until the time that DFCS completed their investigation of this incident. All of the people and the events appeared to be lined up to orchestrate and order our steps in order for us to come to an expected end. Even our son's injury—all that is left is a scar. It reminds us of the day God redirected our lives.

All of these things could not have just happened. There was a greater plan at work to *save us*. Whoever coined the phrase "everything happens for a reason" was on to something because there is no way that this situation should have ended well. Again I submit to you—but God! God had a *master plan*. He knew the *end* before the *beginning*, and He *planned* a better outcome than what the enemy of our soul intended. For, God said, "I know the *plans* I have for you…plans to prosper you and…to give you hope and a future."[1] He could give us this *guarantee* because He already knew how it would end.

"*All things* work together for *good* to them that love God, to them who are the *called* according to His purpose" (Romans 8:28 KJV). We didn't understand it at the time, but we were being called—called by God to come into a wilderness season where we would *experience God* up close and personal.

At this point, there was no turning back. God had captivated our hearts, and we couldn't believe that He loved us so. Prior to this time, we only *really* read about God and His power. Now, we were up front and personal with God, the Creator.

God singlehandedly orchestrated my husband's and our family's salvation. We used to sing a song at church that said, "Salvation has been brought down." This song didn't have much meaning until this happened. We came to the point in our lives where nothing else mattered but to love and serve God. Nothing else mattered because no one else could possibly save us—but God.

This nine-month period of time—from the point of meeting the angel that walked me through this trial that culminated in a forty-day fast until the end of the DFCS investigation—pointed us in the direction of our destiny. We were at a fork in the road where we walked the tightrope of life, having tried to live without God and ultimately falling off the ropes. We were drawn into a twelve-year journey of discovery that began and ended with this question: *Whom do you worship?*

We needed to find a new place of worship because our season was up where we had been worshipping, and we needed direction as to where we were to go from there.

The following weekend, my husband and I attended a 100 Black Men of DeKalb County event. While leaving the event, we got into the elevator with the pastor of Voices of Faith Baptist Church, and he invited us to be his personal guests the next day at their friends-and-family day. God had a plan.

---

1. Jeremiah 29:11.

Getting ready to go to worship the next day was a harrowing experience, to say the least. Our children didn't want to go. They wanted to go to Cornerstone as usual. We gave no explanation—we were just going to visit. But something within me—I believe it was God's Spirit directing me—believed that this would be our next place of worship.

When we got to the doors of the church, everyone greeted us with such love. They hugged us and loved on us. It felt so good receiving that unconditional love, and I was sold on the idea when we came through the front door that this would be home. Then we entered the sanctuary, and the music was excellent and the preaching on point. It just felt right, but I couldn't make a move this fast. My husband and family weren't ready to make a decision to make this our church home without more investigation—or could we? Well, I waited until my husband and family appeared ready to make that step—or maybe I pushed them to make that step.

I tended to be the driver of our spiritual lives…pushing here…pushing there…to make things go the way that I thought was best. Little did I know at the time, but I was driving a wedge between my husband and me.

After a couple of weeks of attendance, we joined the church when they opened the doors for new membership. I was so excited. This church had an incredible music department and very active children's ministry. After going through the church's new-member orientation, I decided to volunteer teaching, and my husband volunteered with the audio/visual department, where he worked the soundboard during worship services.

No, I didn't immediately join the choir. I had heard that they had a very strict tryout for the choir, and I felt that I needed to volunteer in other areas to get to know people first before doing the one thing that I loved the most, so that when I did join the choir, people would *know* my heart.

Teaching ran a second to singing, but I always got a charge from working with children. This experience taught me to be specific in what I wanted to do. I was very general, and I was trying to be accommodating because they appeared to have very few volunteers for the younger children, but my heart was set on teaching the college-age group. There was only one problem—they had more teachers for the college-age group than they had students. Believe it or not, there was a waiting list for teachers for this age group. So, I taught the three- and four-year-olds for about a year. It wore me out. By the end of that year, an opening had come up to team teach the college-age group with a group of three teachers that rotated Sundays.

One Sunday that I was to teach, my lesson was taken from the book of Hosea. Honestly, in my history of being a Christian, I did not study the Old Testament very much. At the most, we studied Psalms and Proverbs. Therefore, I had never read, nor did I have any knowledge of, the book of Hosea. This meant that I had to do extra-intensive study.

In reading the text for the lesson, I began in Hosea 1, and as I read this Scripture, the tears began to flow from my eyes. There was such a parallel in Hosea to my own life. And reading this Scripture caused me to ask questions of God. How could God ask a man to marry someone that He knows will be unfaithful? Who does that? Would God go that far to send a message? Not only did God want Hosea to take an unfaithful bride, but once she became unfaithful, He had Hosea go find her, bring her back to his house, clean her up, and even name the babies that she conceived through her adulterous affairs. This did not sound like a loving and merciful God at all.

As I prepared for this lesson, it became apparent to me that I *really* did not know God like I thought I did. I understood that God was not like man, but this was unusual. But then I had to bring this message home to my own situation. Do I know what it *feels like* to love someone and have them turn their backs on you? They reject your love and your kindness. They give others credit for what you've done for them. While they are at home with you, they are loving to you, but as soon as they walk out the door and leave the house, they take off their wedding ring, or they chase everyone else but their spouse.

Ah…*now* there was a connection. I don't know about you, but I need a connection to what I must teach because I can't convey to others unless I have a deeper understanding. And I knew what it *felt* like to be pushed away—to be broken by those that I loved, those that were the object of my affection.

I was then ready to present this lesson to college-aged students that were just starting their lives. Little did I know that I would have students in the class that had been through some things. Some of them had experienced things that I had not even thought of, let alone experienced—and haven't even now. Needless to say, we had a very lively discussion, and I saw the light bulb come on for many of them. My own recent involvements helped to seal their understanding since I taught from an experiential platform. This builds confidence in the subject matter for the learner because of the light that is shed from the point of view of a participant rather than a spectator.

Much to my dismay, this ended up being the last lesson that I taught at Voices of Faith. The following Saturday, I participated in the open-mic event that was held during the church's anniversary festivities. After singing "In the Midst of It All," made popular by Yolanda Adams, the pastor asked me to sing that song the next morning—at all three worship services.

Needless to say, from that moment on, I was singing in the choir and on the praise team. Teaching was no longer possible because of the travel time between services and locations—not to mention the travel that was required in accompanying our pastor when he was invited to preach at engagements in and around the city and out of town. But I was so excited because the music was fantastic. It gave me the outlet that I was missing.

Our time at Voices of Faith was a time of preparation. Michael and I grew spiritually as well as in business. As we were obedient in all areas, including tithes and offerings, God enlarged our territories. Everything appeared to come easily because God's favor was showered on us. From the outside looking in, everyone saw that we bounced back from all of the negative that had happened and we were moving full steam ahead into our future.

Early one Sunday morning before I was to lead praise and worship, the Lord woke me up around three a.m. by shaking our bed. Initially, I was reluctant to wake up, but because this wasn't the first time that this had occurred,

I knew exactly what was happening. I finally got up and sat on the side of the bed and asked God whom it was that I needed to pray for. I immediately had a vision of a guy whom I had never met. It appeared that this person had gone through a lot of terrible things recently (as of that day of the vision), but God wanted me to let him know that He had plans to turn everything around in his favor.

Then God began to tell me that He had chosen me. I was confused. I knew that all of the things that we had gone through had happened in preparation for something. I just didn't see what it was leading to. Then I perceived the Spirit saying that I was chosen for ministry. The *only* ministry that I could see that would have been possible was music ministry. So I put a box around what I perceived that the Spirit meant: music ministry.

Then Sunday morning came. While leading praise and worship, the Spirit was prompting me to stop singing and announce what had happened to me early in the morning and to say that although things had been really tough for this person, God had a plan to turn everything around for him. While walking down the steps of the stage in order to come closer to the audience, I saw the face of the person from the vision that I'd had during the night. I walked over near him to make sure that he was the same guy that I had seen, and it was—*wow*.

As I turned around to walk back up the stairs, I could see that those that led the praise-and-worship team were furious, but there were others that appeared amazed because this had never happened during worship there before. As we finished and were returning to our seats in the choir stand, I was concerned about what others thought of me. This incident changed me forever, but I was still concerned about the perceptions of others. Nothing quite like this had ever happened…what was I to do with this type of gift? How was I to develop it?

A couple of months went by, and the church held a church-growth conference—and it was a real production. Our church was one of the fastest-growing churches in America. Therefore, it was the pastor's goal to give information to small and new churches on how to develop plans and put systems in place to prepare for and cultivate similar types of growth. So, from education to accounting to finance options, many topics were covered to equip pastors and their leadership teams in building churches.

During the day, there were classes to teach the material by those that were instrumental in setting up systems at the church, and in the evening there was worship. Featured artists and pastors were invited to participate nightly. I had never participated up close in anything quite like it.

It was first class all the way. Speakers included Bishops Eddie Long and I. V. Hilliard, and artists included William Murphy, Tonex, and J. Moss. And the house was packed every night. This all stemmed from excellent leadership.

Our pastor was also being consecrated as bishop at this same conference. What an awe-inspiring experience it was. This was all new to me. I grew up in the Church of Christ, where preachers were called Brother and no one carried a title. There was lots of pomp and circumstance surrounding the consecration ceremony, and I learned a lot about the office of bishop and the whole notion of just how important consecration was.

I got so caught up in all of the celebration and the spectacle of big-named, celebrity-type preachers and artists that it bordered on idol worship. It was only in retrospect that months later I reflected on my own reaction—how I worked hard to make sure that I arrived early to get a good seat when I did not have to sing. And how I made a point of volunteering to sing as many nights as were available to guarantee that I was seated on stage and did not have to sit at the rear of the sanctuary or worse—have to stand. Or sit on the stairs of the stage!

Each night of the conference, there were arrangements and rearrangements to accommodate the celebrities instead of the visitors. As I watched, there was something inside of me that was disturbed by all of the commotion to go above and beyond for those that obviously had more than their fair share of attention. And don't mention our elderly—there were no accommodations for them.

I watched as elderly, tithing members were tossed around the sanctuary to oblige these celebrities, and one elderly woman walked out of the program, humiliated by one of the leaders when asked to move her seat over… and over…and over again.

Yet, I was still consumed by all the activity and was glad to be in the mix. There was a charge in the atmosphere. That energy came from our leaders, who were the visionaries of the church and this conference intended to give back what they had been privy to. Their giving nature was what I loved so much about them.

On one of the final nights of the conference, a well-known prophetess spoke and prophesied regarding church leadership in general. She prophesied that there would be many pastors across the nation that would fall from grace— three of whom were major pastors in the metro-Atlanta area that would fall from their positions. While she was ministering, I had a strange feeling about what she was prophesying. At the time, I couldn't put a finger on what I was feeling, but I knew in my heart that something had shifted for me.

4

I CHOOSE TO REPENT: THE SPIRIT OF ELI LIVES ON

His sons, however, did not listen to their father's rebuke,
for it was the Lord's will to put them to death.

1 SAMUEL 2:25

A little over a month after the church-growth conference, my husband received a referral from a friend who was also a member of our church. A bishop from Detroit, Michigan, was looking for a church in the Atlanta metro area to purchase. At about the same time, he also received a call from a Bishop Powers, who was looking to purchase a home in Atlanta.

My husband ended up playing phone tag for about a month with the bishop from Detroit but actually met several times with Bishop Powers to show him properties for sale. My husband hit it off immediately with Bishop Powers. It wasn't in the height—it was in the *might*—this was a saying of Bishop Powers's because of his size. He was small of stature but was bigger than life in every other way.

Right before Thanksgiving 2004, my husband finally connected with the other bishop, Bishop Jones, and their connection was immediate as well. Bishop Jones, his wife, and their team arranged to travel to Atlanta the following week to scout out properties in order to plant a church in Atlanta. The previous year, God had instructed Bishop Jones to come to Atlanta to start a new work—God had a new assignment for him.

When they arrived, Michael picked them up at their hotel, and he fell in love with them. They were both very charismatic and loved the Lord and His people very deeply. Michael fell in love with them, but he was gun shy because of his perception of church folk.

So, he brought them to the office to meet me. I, too, fell in love with them. In conversation with one of their team members at our office, the topic of the Holy Spirit came up. I was hooked.

After my encounter with the angel that had taught me so much about prayer and the Holy Spirit, I wanted to have the Holy Spirit live in me. So I asked them how to get the Holy Spirit. This sparked the fire that was to be lit from our relationship with them. The team member that I was speaking with went over to the bishop to express to him my request, and he got so excited.

He explained to me that all I had to do was ask for Holy Spirit—that He is a gentleman and that He would not intrude. So I asked, but nothing *appeared* to happen at that time.

We ended up going to dinner with them and their team members, and we had a ball. They really knew how to have a good time, and we connected on so many levels—but still my husband was standoffish because of past experiences.

The following week, my husband had an appointment to meet with Bishop Powers to show him properties. After showing the last house to him, while still in the last house, Bishop Powers turned to Michael and began to share some things with him. He told him that God had shown him some of the things that he had done and that God forgave him—of *everything*.

He told him that a *spiritual giant* was trying to *connect* with him. He said that God wanted him to go with this spiritual giant and that God had a plan for his life. Michael understood exactly what he meant by this.

My husband came back to the office after this encounter, and as he was telling me what had happened, we both cried and held each other. He could not believe what had transpired. He was overwhelmed by God's lovingkindness toward him—amazing what a difference a day makes! He knew that only God could have revealed all of those things to him, but he had *never* encountered anyone like Bishop Powers. He told him all about his life and then shared their similarities.

He learned that Bishop Powers's mother shared Michael's birthday and that Bishop Powers's birthday was the same as our oldest son, June 4, but there were fifty years between them. He also found out that Bishop Powers was born in the same year as my mother. God had a plan. Bishop Powers became more of a father to my husband and me beginning on that day.

After this, our lives moved very quickly. Bishop Jones called my husband and told him that they were going to sponsor our first trip to Detroit to visit their church. They thought that it would be good for us to see their facilities and to meet some of their members to get a feel for their ministry.

We were set to travel on the morning of December 16, 2004. We were both excited because we didn't have to do anything. The only plan we had to make was to arrange for coverage at the office while we were away. We had an awesome team working for us, so this was not a problem. Bishop Jones's travel agent arranged for us to be picked up by limousine from the airport once we arrived in Detroit. Then we were on to the bishop's mansion.

We were on our way. In my mind, I was focused on receiving the Holy Spirit—nothing else mattered to me. I knew Michael would handle the business aspects because that was what he was an expert at. But after all that we had been through, I knew that I didn't want to live another day without Him—the Holy Spirit.

At the bishop's mansion, we received a tour of the mansion, and then lunch that was prepared by "Granny." Granny was Bishop Jones's mother-in-law, and she would soon become our family as well. Granny was special in so many ways, but most importantly, she had a real servant's heart. She and everyone else that we encountered that was associated with the church were so loving and cared for our every need. Even on the way from the airport, the driver wouldn't allow me to pay for a Tylenol.

Their service to us was first class all the way. They rolled out the red carpet. The house was decorated for Christmas and was filled with Christmas cheer. They even had prepared an itinerary for us to have things to do while we were there. Every meal was paid for by the bishop. Even the events that we attended outside of church attendance were paid for by him.

We were blown away by their kindness. They had only met us less than thirty days before, but they treated us like we were special and already a part of the family. That Friday night, we attended a "miracle service." When we arrived, we were ushered to the front row as personal guests of the bishop.

Michael and I were in the midst of intense worship when we both felt a strong wind blow over our heads. We looked at each other. "Did you feel that?" my husband asked me. "Yes!" was my reply. What was that? Better still, who was that?

My husband looked above us and all around and noticed that there wasn't a vent overhead. No fan—nothing to indicate that we should've felt a wind blowing over us. We were intrigued to say the least. Was that the *Holy Spirit*?

From that point on, we kept our eyes open to see what was happening. Later that night, the bishop arranged for us to meet Sister Dorothy. She was the bishop's personal intercessor and a member of the leadership team. She became my spiritual midwife of sorts.

The next day, I met with Sister Dorothy, and she spent time with me, teaching me about the importance of the Holy Spirit and His role in our salvation. She explained that you can be saved and never receive the Holy Spirit. But to completely live a holy life, we need the Holy Spirit.

I hung on to her every word because with each word that she spoke, I found new life that sprung up in me. It was as if I was anticipating the things that took place.

Then she took me into an office space in the church, and she began praying in tongues. She instructed me to ask again for the Holy Spirit to live in me. So, I did as she instructed me. Even though she instructed, it was my desire to be filled with His Spirit. We stayed in that room for hours, waiting on me to receive Him.

It was obvious that my mind and my spirit were working against each other. I was trying to wrap my brain around this whole notion of receiving the Holy Spirit instead of just letting go to receive Him. But, as a midwife does, she prompted me to keep pushing.

Then it happened. I was calling, "Jesus, Jesus, Jesus, Jesus, Jesus!" I then fell to the ground weeping as I began speaking in tongues. It took me a while to get up from the floor. It wasn't as I had expected it—it was subtle but certain. The Spirit was there.

That Sunday, we ate dinner with the bishop's family. Granny prepared some things for us to carry with us, and we headed to the airport to travel back to Atlanta. But deep down inside, we really didn't want to leave. We had found a new family.

While waiting to board the plane, Michael and I discussed the weekend events, and we were simply amazed. We realized that what we had experienced was set up by God to bless us. But why us? My husband's response was, "Why not us?" Although we had been far from perfect Christians, why wouldn't God want to bless us?

I was raised to think that Christianity carried with it a certain element of piety and humility that involved serving but not receiving. Although I believed that you reap what you sow, I didn't equate that with my serving. My expectation was that you serve without expecting anything in return for it. So needless to say, I was overwhelmed by the way that everyone wanted to serve us.

After that weekend, we began a year of traveling to Detroit every other weekend—at the expense of the bishop. The bishop said that he was being led by God to do this for us. This surprised us because we had not even committed to the church yet—we were still members of our church in Georgia.

Because of our regular visits, they gave us our own room in the bishop's mansion. During that year, we got to spend lots of one-on-one time with the bishop and his wife, and they poured so much into us as a married couple in ministry as well as spiritually—how to flow in the supernatural.

Bishop Jones and his wife made the decision to begin having Wednesday-night services at a local hall near our home. They also began a weekly television broadcast locally so that people in the area would know that they were in town.

Each week, they, along with their team, flew into Hartsfield International Airport on Wednesday morning, held services, had dinner, stayed overnight at a local hotel, and flew out the next morning back to Detroit. The team that travelled with them included administrative staff, prayer ministers, musicians—or minstrels, as they were called—elders, and other church leadership.

Miracles were happening every week. All types of conditions were healed—the deaf began to hear; cancer was cured without chemo; a former professional athlete who suffered from multiple sclerosis and was unable to walk began walking and a few months later was able to drive again after attending one of these services. Word spread about the miracles and that people were being saved, delivered, healed, and set free.

After a few months, we were outgrowing the hall that had a maximum capacity of approximately three hundred. This prompted the bishop to look with more resolve for a permanent location, always praying to God for His direction.

One night during that particular time, I had a dream that we were in a church building with the bishop, having worship services. The dream was almost as if we were watching a virtual tour of the building. I never saw the exterior of the building in my dream. But I could see the stair hallway on both ends of the building and I saw the sanctuary, but not as it was when we first saw the building. What I saw in the dream was the sanctuary after renovations had been completed. I shared my dream with the bishop, and he said that we must be getting close to finding the right building. So, we looked with more urgency.

At each Wednesday-night service, the bishop would announce that we were looking for a building, but we got no more information from members or visitors than what we were able to find through our real estate sources online. Then my husband happened upon a building that had been a fore-closure but an investor had purchased it and had it up for sale.

We met the realtor at the building, and it just so happened to be a woman that had been attending our Wednesday-night miracle services. The bishop asked her why she had not given us the information about that building, since she was the listing agent, but she had no real explanation.

We found out that the original owners of the building had been the First Church of the Nazarene, but after they sold the building, there had been several churches in that building that had lots of issues, e.g., pastors that ran off with money and pastors that were doing all types of evil things to their members, etc. But everyone really liked the building, especially the bishop and his wife. Therefore, they put in an offer to purchase the property.

Unfortunately, all of the lending offers for financing the church were very unfavorable. My husband then suggested that we ask the owner to provide owner financing for a period of time that would be mutually beneficial to all parties, and this idea was presented to the owner.

The owner didn't object to any of the terms and in fact agreed to all terms offered. That meant that we had a permanent location. In less than six months from our first Wednesday-night miracle service, we were in our own building.

This meant that the prayer team from the mother church needed to travel to the new building to pray and consecrate it because of all of the negative and evil things that had transpired there. The prayer team stayed at the new building for a week, and the evangelism team came along to canvass the neighborhood.

Again, miracles were happening every week, but much ground had to be "broken up" in regard to setting the *atmosphere* for true transformation to take place in the lives of the people. Setting the atmosphere required a specific set of procedures that, if put into practical use, could transform any life. The main ingredient was prayer. Any church with its foundation stabilized by prayer stands firm through tests and trials, and this ministry set the bar high in this area.

Another essential element was worship preparation. Again, this involved daily prayer and intercession, preparing worship leaders on how to go into warfare with the music, and lots and lots of teaching. Effective leadership played a major role in the accomplishment of this task. The bishop's wife was instrumental in the development of the music ministry. Because of her passion for the arts and how music affects all facets of the supernatural administration, she allowed Holy Spirit to move in ways that most churches never experience, and that is through the introduction of "the song of the Lord." At almost every worship service, through the work of the minstrels and praise leaders, Holy Spirit would produce a new song. This is why they called their musicians minstrels instead of musicians—because of their relationship with Holy Spirit.

Musicians are hired hands, but minstrels have a heart like David, where music *is* the worship and not just an *enhancement* to the worship. They are *anointed* by God to do what they do, and it is reflected in the music that is produced. Of course, there is a level of consecration that takes place in order for minstrels to operate at a level where heaven invades the worship—and that is why the bishop and his wife travelled with minstrels that carried that consecration and anointing.

This was a daunting task, to say the least—to sponsor travel for at least ten people every week, plus their own travel expenses, in order to plant a new church in a new city. Once the location had been secured, a decision had to be made as to who from the mother church would move to Atlanta in order to facilitate the training and development of new church leaders. They needed to be dedicated to the work ahead but also have the heart of the bishop. After much prayer, the bishop announced those that would move to the Atlanta area from the mother church to assist in the development of new leaders. These people would be available in all areas of ministry, but the bishop would continue to travel back and forth to minister weekly.

Initially, it worked out okay for the bishop and his wife to travel back and forth. They secured an apartment locally and completed renovations to the church building to accommodate offices for both of them. But as time went on, it became very taxing on them and their family time—there were birthdays, holidays, special occasions that came up and even vacations that had not been factored into the equation of a new church plant. In order to keep things going, the bishop made a schedule for some of the pastors from the mother church to travel weekly to Atlanta to minister in his stead.

This is when things began to fall apart. Everyone that was sent didn't have the same heart or anointing as the bishop, and the people that attended services left disappointed. The same thing was happening at the mother church. Members would call the church to see if the bishop was going to be there on that upcoming Sunday, and the response would be yes, but that meant that he would be there in the spirit! These people would attend on that following Sunday only to be disappointed that the bishop was not there, and they would leave.

Offerings declined at the mother church on the Sundays that the bishop was in Atlanta and vice versa. He was trying to prop up this project because it became too big for him to do on his own. But finding those whom God had chosen to walk this out with him was the missing link. By all indications, the bishop was backpedaling, trying to find a more suitable solution to do what God had told him to do.

On the weeks that they knew the bishop was coming to Atlanta, his Atlanta team would jump around, trying to do the things that they should have been doing consistently every week. They were ill-equipped in the area of leading in ministry and had no idea what it took to meet the needs of the people. Even the basic, everyday, run-of-the-mill work that shouldn't require any high level of thinking went undone until someone told them that it needed to be done. Then they would try to push those tasks off on someone else. They just didn't have the heart of the bishop.

What was missing in Atlanta was leadership. Part-time leadership doesn't work well for any church, especially a new church plant. We had no one that had been appointed to move to Atlanta that would take ownership of the role of leading in the place of the bishop. Therefore, the growth that was realized early on was stifled.

Michael and I were encouraged to register for the upcoming catechism classes, and eventually prophecy and healing-the-sick classes were offered, and everyone lined up to participate. There was *a hunger for more* in those that took part in these classes. But those that taught the catechism classes appeared ill prepared for the level of questions that were asked of them. During one particular catechism-class session, a woman asked for clarification on the Triune God and how it was possible for the three distinct personalities, the Father, the Son, and the Holy Spirit, to be *one God*. The elder that was teaching the class gave the following example: The Triune God is the equivalent of Eddie Murphy playing all of the parts in *The Nutty Professor*. But this didn't make sense because all of those fictitious characters that he portrayed were not the same people at any point in time—the actor playing all of the parts was the same individual. This caused quite a bit of confusion and talk among the new members—so much so that this same elder was called to the bishop to report on what went wrong.

Unfortunately, the bishop had to fly in to correct several things at that same time, and this was one of the things that he had to address. In teaching on the Trinity, the bishop gave the example of himself—he was husband, father, and son, but he was one and the same person. These roles characterized who he was in any given circumstance. As a husband, he carried a different demeanor than he did as a father, but because he was one and the same person in every instance, his character and responses were always consistent. As he was explaining this to the audience, you could see his frustration and discontent with having to always circle back to cover those that he had chosen to carry the Atlanta church. He knew something had to change—there just weren't any clear solutions apparent to him at that point.

We all were hard-pressed to come up with a solution to the bishop needing to be in two places at one time because of the struggle that came from juggling both locations. Our oldest son, who was and is always exploring cutting-edge technology, shared with one of the elders the latest technology at the time, which was simulcast. Simulcasting is the broadcasting of programs or events across more than one medium or more than one service on the same medium at exactly the same time—in essence, simultaneous broadcasting. This elder shared this with the bishop, but instead of giving credit where credit was due, he said it was his own idea and not our son's. Nevertheless, the bishop pushed to implement simulcasting immediately.

Simulcasting seemed to be the perfect solution to the problem of managing being at two places at one time. But the reality of this ministry was that if you had sheep looking for a shepherd, simulcasting was too impersonal. Yeah, there are people that come to a place of worship to blend in with the group. That's why a lot of times multi-site churches will grow to extreme numbers—some in the tens of thousands—while simulcasting or showing film of past messages to its weekly membership. This is because it meets a need for them—it will not be said that they are not church goers! Then there are those that like the celebrity preacher that is the pastor of the church, and that is the draw for them. What we have found is that those people don't want to be seen. They want to be counted in the number—to say that they are members of a megachurch, but they don't get involved. They have a righteousness of their own, but they are lost. They are sheep without a shepherd. Many of them really do want to connect on a more intimate level and with accountability, but that would mean removing their masks, and for many that's way too painful to imagine. That would leave them too vulnerable for comfort, and others would see who they really are.

Funny thing though—we didn't seem to have that problem. Those that came to worship with us were looking for a more intimate relationship. They were sheep *looking* for a shepherd.

Additionally, the miracles that we all had become accustomed to were not as effective on screen as seeing them live and in person. Therefore, the simulcast idea was a total flop. No one liked it. Now we were back to square one. What do we do about the problem of the bishop being in two places at one time?

During this time, the bishop and his family went on vacation. When they returned, the bishop announced that he was going to move a pastor from the mother church to Atlanta to be an administrative pastor, but he would still preside as bishop.

On hearing this, my husband was skeptical. For a year and a half, the bishop had grown the ministry based on himself. All media and television broadcast was of him—not this new pastor. Now he was shifting gears. Was he setting this up to fail? How eager would everyone be about a new leader totally unknown to them? Even with mixed emotions and reservations, we all rallied around the idea, giving our full support to the bishop. We knew that he was in a tough position, and we didn't want our skepticism to make his decisions any tougher than they already were.

The new pastor and his family moved to Atlanta, and we had the arduous task of starting all over again. They moved during the Thanksgiving/Christmas holiday season and had no one in Atlanta, so our family spent as much time with them as possible to help them acclimate during the hardest time of the year to leave everyone and everything that they held dear.

The beautiful thing was that they didn't have to worry about any expenses. Everything—from the rent on their new home to all expenses to run the church—was paid for by the mother church. All they had to do was work to grow the church—take what had already been started and develop it by cultivating the same atmosphere conducive for miracles to happen.

The first issue was that this pastor tried to be the bishop instead of authentically becoming who God wanted him to be. He had been under the bishop's ministry since he was a child, and he had witnessed the bishop grow the church in Detroit. During those years, there were many ups and downs and a huge learning curve for the bishop regarding dealing with people in ministry.

But the makeup of the church that the bishop took over was vastly different from the church plant in Atlanta. The people that gravitated to the church in Atlanta were true to our Southern roots in the Bible belt. We unapologetically attended church services, and we were very knowledgeable of the Word of God. This new pastor and those that moved from the mother church *assumed* that we (those dumb Southerners) didn't have a clue regarding the Word and had to be taught how to serve God. We were considered babes although many of the members had been Christians all of our lives—and many were well into their sixties.

True leaders observe first then act upon what they have observed. They seldom *assume*. This new pastor assumed based on all that he had heard that he needed to come in just to preach. His estimation was that all of the leg work had been done in establishing the work there, that the relationships had been developed, and all he needed to do was just coast along. He did not realize that when he got there, we were really starting over—from ground zero.

The bishop authentically developed into the leader that he was by trial and error and through a close walk with the Holy Spirit. He did not mimic anyone else. What you saw was what you got. He was not a phony. But because he had become bigger than life due to all of his accomplishments, most people in the ministry thought that it was safest to just follow his path rather than forge their own, relying on the Holy Spirit to create something new through them.

It went from bad to worse. The weekly sermons became more and more browbeating instead of uplifting and less about seeing people healed, delivered, and set free. Because of this, my husband grew weary of the treatment that we received at the hands of the new pastor. He was trying to force my husband and me to serve in capacities that we felt should be opened to other members so that we got full participation. But, the pastor saw this as insurrection, disobedience, and disrespect—we were telling him no. He thought that it was preposterous to say no to your pastor. As if he were *equal* with God!

If you didn't serve him the way that he thought that you ought to, you were considered an outsider and treated as such. Therefore, many people, out of a need to belong, did exactly what he wanted. They all but bowed in his presence. Didn't Jesus Christ say, "I came to *serve*, not to be served"?

During worship services (although the bishop and his wife were not in attendance), they would have everyone stand, clap, and recognize them by acknowledging their chairs that were on stage. Those *chairs* were considered sacred. No one could even touch those chairs—not for any reason. I knew, based on conversations with the bishop's wife very early on in our membership there, that witches were putting curses on the chairs. Therefore, most of the leaders were guarded regarding their chairs. But this went beyond protecting their anointing—this bordered on *idol worship*.

We began to shift in our devotion to the ministry—there were conflicts for us. During Shepherd's Day Celebration that year, services were simulcast so that both churches could celebrate "together." Shepherd's Day, even from the beginning of our membership there, created a conflict for me. There was so much pomp and circumstance, and more than normal amounts of planning went into the orchestration of this day—every year! But during this particular service, as I was watching, I heard the Spirit of God say, "They don't do this much planning and celebrating when they worship Me…" Was the Spirit saying that we were worshipping the bishop and his wife?

We saw the first set of church members leave. After they left, the sermons turned gruesome in nature. The pastor began cursing them by saying that their lives would fall apart because they were leaving the ministry. He said that their marriages would fail—that their children would rebel against them—all sorts of foolishness.

But you *cannot* curse what God has blessed. Those that stayed would look for any news that pointed to trouble in the lives of those that were leaving. They would tell stories about people that left the mother church during the Bishop's early ministry—how some got deathly ill and came back needing the bishop to pray for them. Some were killed, and others experienced divorce, financial loss, etc.

Who would sit around and discuss this type of nonsense? This was borderline demonic, and I wanted no part of it. It just didn't sound natural and was sort of scary, except I know in *whom* I have believed. *Christ* died for us—not the bishop. Leaving this church *did not mean* leaving God.

It was obvious that the leadership was using this in order to scare us. They wanted us scared straight to keep us in line, obedient, and fearful of leaving—as if by leaving the church you were leaving God Himself. They wanted that sense of control over us, and many fell for it.

Christ died for us—not the bishop.
Leaving this church *did not mean* leaving God.

One Sunday morning after praise and worship, we again were subjected to hearing another sermon stressing the fact that if we left the ministry we would all be cursed. This time, the minstrels began playing a lament, and as they played, I began to hum to the music—it was better to hum along to this music than to bear listening to the nonsense that the pastor called a sermon. A deep, mournful sound was coming from me, and I didn't know where it was coming from. They were raw, dark, dreadful sounds, and I felt the way that this humming sounded. As I looked up, I locked my gaze with the pastor's for more than what was comfortable for him. Then he got louder and more pronounced with his message. As I sat there, I realized that our season there was over.

As I was leaving to go assist in the finance room to count the collection raised that morning, I tried to figure out a way to tell them that I was resigning from my duties in this area. When we got to the room to count, we prayed and performed our duties as usual. Once we finished, the finance-ministry lead for Atlanta asked me to remain afterward because she wanted to discuss something with me.

She told me that she was sensing that God was leading me to do some other things in the ministry and that she didn't want to hold me back from what God was calling me to. She told me that she would convey this to the bishop and that I should not feel any more obligation to continue beyond that day. Wow! God took care of this without me having to say one word. I was convinced more than ever that our time was up.

The next week, the pastor had several meetings that he requested that my husband sit in on with him. After the meetings ended, he asked my husband to be his armor bearer once again, and as he had on every other occasion, my husband declined. But this time, the pastor became belligerent with him, demanding an explanation. At that moment, one of our friends, Alvin, was waiting on Michael so that they could ride home together, and one of the elders was still at the building. The discussion got so heated that Alvin knocked on the door to see what was going on.

This interaction was so out of hand that they continued their debate in front of Alvin and the other elder. The pastor accused Michael of not looking out for the best interest of the ministry, and Michael and Alvin stormed out instead of allowing this to cause them to disrespect his position as pastor.

On his way home from this meeting, Michael called the bishop to give him a heads-up on what had happened and that he felt he and the pastor needed to have a meeting with an unbiased third party to try to resolve their issues. The bishop agreed with him and set up a meeting with Michael, the pastor, the prayer-ministry leader, and myself.

In the meeting, a lot of petty things were brought up with regard to the pastor's position in asking us to serve in capacities that we felt should be offered to other members in order to get more participation in all areas of ministry. We did not want anyone to think that we were receiving preferential treatment because of our familiarity with the mother church. But it appeared to be more about the pastor's insecurity about whether or not we would have allegiance to him versus our allegiance to the bishop. We didn't understand the need for competition. Whether there was one, two, or thirty churches under one umbrella, we considered it still *one church*. Our stance was that we would not compete—we completed each other. For, where one of us was weak, the other was strong, and together we would be an unbreakable force.

Competition gave us something to be concerned about. And we were not used to leadership trying to force their position on us to make us do what we did not want to do. It was clear that a spirit other than God's Spirit was at work to keep us at odds with each other.

Then it all turned very petty. They questioned whether or not Michael was participating during worship services. The pastor claimed that there were others that told him that during worship, Michael would be on his phone instead of following along when the congregation was reading Scripture. Michael explained that his Bible was on his phone—that's why he was on the phone.

Then Michael shared his concern regarding the need for us to worship the chairs that the bishop and his wife sat in even when they were not in attendance. He told them, "It's only a *chair!* The bishop's anointing is *not* in the chair—it's in the *man!* If this building burns down tonight and those chairs burn down with the building, the bishop will *still* carry the anointing. Those chairs are inanimate objects. God lives in living things!"

As we left that meeting, I saw Michael with a new level of respect. He did not disrespect the pastor's position, but he also did not allow them to demean his understanding of who God is and the place that He alone deserves in our hearts and in our worship. He stood firm and exerted his position on the fact that what they wanted us to do was the equivalent of *idol worship* and we could not participate in that.

I was proud of him. It reminded me of the three Hebrew boys that refused to bow down that we read about over in Daniel 3. He made no apologies for his position, and it left them speechless.

Michael knew that they would call the bishop before he could, but he called him anyway to let him know that they'd had their meeting. The bishop thought that because of some things that Michael had brought up in the meeting that he would meet with the entire congregation to ascertain if this was the consensus of everyone else. But before meeting with the congregation, the bishop met with Michael one-on-one because of their relationship. He loved Michael like a son and was concerned about him.

That's what I loved about the bishop—he really had a heart for people. This whole interaction caused him to be torn—the politics of religion put him in a position of having to choose sides, but his role as a spiritual father caused him to care for each individually, understanding that there was a greater power at work to destroy God's original plan. His plan was unity above all else and the preservation of relationships.

But Michael was at a crossroads—follow man or follow God as He redirects him to his destiny. Whether anyone knew what he had been through to get to God was irrelevant at this point—he knew what he had been through. Overcoming every obstacle was no accident. God had orchestrated this. And Michael was choosing to forge a new path—a road that he had never travelled before—but he was confident that the way would be made for him by a power that was able to do it. And that was God's power to save.

As fate would have it, the meeting with the congregation produced nothing but a line in the sand. There were finger pointing and accusations by the pastor and those that had received in their hearts that which this pastor had spoken over them Sunday after Sunday—that they would be cursed if they left the ministry. These people stood in agreement with the pastor out of fear.

Michael walked out of the meeting without saying another word. It was time to exit. But you could see the hurt in the bishop's face.

The next week, without a new place to worship, I came back to what was comfortable. I don't really know why I did this except that it's always hard for me to break ties with people and places. While in worship, I heard the Spirit of God say, "Tell the bishop that the spirit of Eli lives on, and I AM cursing this ministry because he will not discipline his spiritual sons."

"Who am I to tell the bishop this, Lord?" I asked of God. Of course, I did not immediately obey God in doing this. I waited a couple of days, trying to process these statements. When I did call the bishop to tell him this, his response was, "That is *not* God!"

How could he say this? He and his wife had both *trained* me, but beyond training, they knew that God had spoken to me on their behalf on numerous occasions, and at every one of those times, they felt it was accurate. Why the change of heart? Was it because it was a difficult word to receive? Or was it because it did not edify or exalt them in any way, shape, or form?

I obeyed God, but my heart was torn in pieces. We both loved the bishop and his family as our own family. This rendered us immobile—we couldn't move—but God did…

A week or so later, Michael received a call from the bishop's sister. She called the bishop prior to calling Michael in order to get permission to speak with him, and permission was granted. She asked Michael if he was okay, and she proceeded to tell him about a dream that she had regarding Michael and the pastor in Atlanta. She confirmed all that Michael had been going through because God had showed it to her in a dream. She prayed with Michael and said that she would speak with the bishop to appeal to him regarding their conversation. But he never heard back from her or from the bishop.

The next week, Bishop Powers called Michael from New York City. He was scheduled to come into town and wanted to meet with him. Michael picked up Bishop Powers, and we went to Piccadilly Restaurant for lunch. This was my first time meeting him, and I was amazed.

He and Michael spent time catching up on all of Bishop Powers's travels since they had last seen each other. Bishop Powers, as an apostle, was a world traveler, and miracles followed everywhere he went.

While eating, Bishop Powers, never hearing anything about what had happened at our previous church, announced to both of us that God was calling us into ministry. He had already seen in the spirit what had transpired, and God was revealing His plan for us in that moment.

We sat with our mouths wide open in total disbelief. It was never our plan or desire to be in ministry—why would God call us?

A month or so after leaving our previous church, the prayer-ministry leader moved to a new apartment and asked us to help her move. Of course, we would not let anything keep us from helping her. She was such a beautiful person—how could we not help her?

While helping to box up some of her things, this sister received a call from the bishop. She walked into her bathroom in order to speak to the bishop in private. But we were still able to hear much of her conversation. She was describing to the bishop what had happened to her earlier that day while directing the daily morning prayer at the church building. Obviously, she had encountered an evil spirit that was *"hovering over"* the sanctuary while she and the others were praying. She said that all of her attempts at calling on the name of Jesus did not move this spirit. After hearing this, the bishop decided that he would fly in their prayer team to pray and consecrate the building once again.

It was obvious that she did not want Michael and me to hear this because of what God had shown me, and I was certain that the bishop shared with her what I'd told him. I knew that God wanted me to hear this only to confirm for me that what I'd heard God say was *real*. This spirit that she saw and encountered was not demonic in nature. God sent it!

5

I CHOOSE TO SUBMIT: BROKEN INTIMACY

If fear is the great enemy of intimacy, love is its true friend.

HENRI NOUWEN

Sex…we can't live without it. But there certainly are a lot of us abusing it instead of cherishing the right to participate in it. The intimate act of sexual intercourse is sacred and should only take place between those in a covenant relationship. The covenant is between the man, woman, and God. In every covenant that God makes, there are promises that He makes, and marriage is no different.

In making any relationship work, there must be mutual respect, effective communication, and a willingness to work on issues and problems, and you must have trust. Most marriages have gone through stages where one or the other spouse feels that they have been disrespected, lost communication, or are no longer willing to work out problems. This is evident in the number of divorces that are granted every year. Family court is full of married people that just couldn't make it work—for whatever reason. Even on television, you have *Divorce Court*, where individuals come on the show and air out all of their dirty laundry. Most times, there is cheating or infidelity and loss of trust between the two.

Even in the political arena, we see those in elected offices abuse the power that is gained by their position. So much disdain for the marital bed. Then they point fingers at their colleagues, when they are committing far worse offenses.

I realized, though, that as I was fighting to save my own marriage, God is also fighting to save the relationship between Christ and His Bride. He is literally causing havoc to get our attention—to compel us to stay in right relationship with Him.

God made covenants historically—with Adam, Noah, Abraham, Moses, David—and now, through our Lord Jesus Christ, God has given us a new and perpetual covenant. All of these covenants have a common denominator— God's desire to find *one person* that will forsake everything else and follow after Him at all cost, because God wants to be one with His creation. These covenants came out of God's frustration with disobedient man.

The fruits of these covenants gave physical evidence of what God would do for *all* of mankind, if they, too, chose to follow Him. God never intended for us to put these individuals on pedestals where no one else resides. He only wanted to give examples for us to reach for.

The Adamic covenant was God's agreement with Adam to secure his wellbeing in the Garden of Eden. The benefits to Adam and Eve were that they would be fruitful, have power to subdue the earth, and have dominion over all living things that move upon the earth. Disobedience to the covenant by Adam and Eve cost them everything—even their very lives as they knew it. The spiritual death is just as devastating as physical death.

Whenever God determines to bless us, Satan comes to take us off course. Satan knew that Adam and Eve's disobedience would destroy their intimate relationship with God, and thereby he could gain control of their lives.

The Noahic covenant was God's agreement with Noah to provide safety for Noah and his family and a remnant of animals. God gave Noah specific instructions on how to construct the ark. In Genesis 6:13–14 and 17–18, we read:

> *God said to Noah, "I AM going to put an end to all people, for the earth is filled with violence because of them. I AM surely going to destroy both them and the earth. So make yourself an ark of cypress wood; make rooms in it and coat it with pitch inside and out.... I AM going to bring floodwaters on the earth to destroy all life under the heavens, every creature that has the breath of life in it. Everything on earth will perish. But I will establish My covenant with you, and you will enter the ark—you and your sons and your wife and your sons' wives with you."*

Why would God make such a covenant with one man? Had Noah done or established something that set him apart from every other man? Absolutely! Noah was known to walk with God. His desire was intimacy with God. Which is *exactly* what God was seeking—a man that wanted to *know* Him.

But was it just because of his relationship with God? I submit to you that God was sickened by the state of affairs of man. Genesis 6:5–6 reads:

> *The LORD saw how great the wickedness of the human race had become on the earth, and that every inclination of the thoughts of the human heart was only evil all the time. The LORD regretted that He had made human beings on the earth, and His heart was deeply troubled.*

I find it interesting that God was very precise in all of the details of building the ark and the number of animals to include on the ark—that they had to take seven of every clean animal, seven of every kind of bird, but only two of unclean animals. Numbers are very important to God, and seven is the number of completion.

Noah and his family were on the ark exactly seven days before the floods began. They didn't even have to close the door—God did it. When God establishes a covenant, He carries out the details, and the details are complete as the use of the number seven signifies.

But what about the Abrahamic covenant? I mean, it just didn't make sense for God to choose Abram. Abram came from a family with a long history of idol worship. In our time, this would be the equivalent to him being a Muslim or an atheist. Yet God chose Abram—plucked him out from among his family—to establish His covenant with him and to make him the father of Israel and Arab nations.

First, God had to move Abram from his family—the old way of thinking—so that He could establish a relationship with him. Genesis 12:1–3 (NKJV) reads:

> *Now the LORD had said to Abram: "Get out of your country, from your family and from your father's house, to a land that I will show you. I will make you a great nation; I will bless you and make your name great; and you shall be a blessing. I will bless those who bless you, and I will curse him who curses you; and in you all the families of the earth shall be blessed."*

God made several promises to Abraham and his seed. They were:

1. I will make you a great nation.

2. I will bless you.

3. I will make your name great.

4. You will be a blessing.

5. I will bless those that bless you.

6. I will curse those that curse you.

7. All the families of the earth will be blessed through you.

8. I will give Canaan to your seed forever.

9. Your descendants will be as plentiful as the dust of the earth and the stars of the heavens.

10. You will be the father of many nations.

11. Kings will come from you.

12. Your descendants will be victors over their enemies.

These promises are significant because they are now to those that accept Jesus Christ as their Lord and Savior. Galatians 3:2–29 (MSG) states:

> *Let me put this question to you: How did your new life begin? Was it by working your heads off to please God? Or was it by responding to God's Message to you? Are you going to continue this craziness? For only crazy people would think they could complete by their own efforts what was begun by God. If you weren't smart enough or strong enough to begin it, how do you suppose you could perfect it? Did you go through this whole painful learning process for nothing? It is not yet a total loss, but it certainly will be if you keep this up!*
>
> *Answer this question: Does the God who lavishly provides you with His own presence, His Holy Spirit, working things in your lives you could never do for yourselves, does He do these things because of your strenuous moral striving or because you trust Him to do them in you? Don't these things happen among you just as they happened with Abraham? He believed God, and that act of belief was turned into a life that was right with God.*
>
> *Is it not obvious to you that persons who put their trust in Christ (not persons who put their trust in the law!) are like Abraham: children of faith? It was all laid out beforehand in Scripture that God would set things right with non-Jews by faith. Scripture anticipated this in the promise to Abraham: "All nations will be blessed in you."*
>
> *So those now who live by faith are blessed along with Abraham, who lived by faith—this is no new doctrine! And that means that anyone*

who tries to live by his own effort, independent of God, is doomed to failure. Scripture backs this up: "Utterly cursed is every person who fails to carry out every detail written in the Book of the law."

The obvious impossibility of carrying out such a moral program should make it plain that no one can sustain a relationship with God that way. The person who lives in right relationship with God does it by embracing what God arranges for him. Doing things for God is the opposite of entering into what God does for you. Habakkuk had it right: "The person who believes God, is set right by God—and that's the real life." Rule-keeping does not naturally evolve into living by faith, but only perpetuates itself in more and more rule-keeping, a fact observed in Scripture: "The one who does these things [rule-keeping] continues to live by them."

Christ redeemed us from that self-defeating, cursed life by absorbing it completely into Himself. Do you remember the Scripture that says, "Cursed is everyone who hangs on a tree"? That is what happened when Jesus was nailed to the cross: He became a curse, and at the same time dissolved the curse. And now, because of that, the air is cleared and we can see that Abraham's blessing is present and available for non-Jews, too. We are all able to receive God's life, His Spirit, in and with us by believing—just the way Abraham received it.

Friends, let me give you an example from everyday affairs of the free life I am talking about. Once a person's will has been signed, no one else can annul it or add to it. Now, the promises were made to Abraham and to his descendant. You will observe that Scripture, in the careful language of a legal document, does not say "to descendants," referring to everybody in general, but "to your descendant" (the noun, note, is singular), referring to Christ. This is the way I interpret this: A will, earlier signed by God, is not annulled by an addendum attached 430 years later, thereby negating the promise of the will. No, this addendum, with its instructions and regulations, has nothing to do with the promised inheritance in the will.

What is the point, then, of the law, the attached addendum? It was a thoughtful addition to the original covenant promises made to Abraham. The purpose of the law was to keep a sinful people in the way of salvation until Christ (the descendant) came, inheriting the promises and distributing them to us. Obviously this law was not a firsthand encounter with God. It was arranged by angelic messengers through a middleman, Moses. But if there is a middleman as there was at Sinai, then the people are not dealing directly with God, are they? But the original promise is the direct blessing of God, received by faith.

If such is the case, is the law, then, an anti-promise, a negation of God's will for us? Not at all. Its purpose was to make obvious to everyone that we are, in ourselves, out of right relationship with God, and therefore to show us the futility of devising some religious system for getting by our own efforts what we can only get by waiting in faith for God to complete His promise. For if any kind of rule-keeping had power to create life in us, we would certainly have gotten it by this time.

Until the time when we were mature enough to respond freely in faith to the living God, we were carefully surrounded and protected by the Mosaic Law. The law was like those Greek tutors, with which you are familiar, who escort children to school and protect them from danger or distraction, making sure the children will really get to the place they set out for.

But now you have arrived at your destination: By faith in Christ you are in direct relationship with God. Your baptism in Christ was not just washing you up for a fresh start. It also involved dressing you in an adult faith wardrobe—Christ's life, the fulfillment of God's original promise.

In Christ's family there can be no division into Jew and non-Jew, slave
and free, male and female. Among us you are all equal. That is, we
are all in a common relationship with Jesus Christ. Also, since you
are Christ's family, then you are Abraham's famous "descendant," heirs
according to the covenant promises.

It's because of covenant that I won't throw in the towel on my marriage—
God is still at the center of it. As I stated before, my husband has struggled
in his faithfulness to me. Today, he sent me an email: "I was just thinking
of you...miss you..." Isn't it amazing that a man can lavish you with his
words, but love is not at the root of his affections or intentions? If he were
exposed for who he really is, he would become angry and accuse me of being
a jealous woman. But is there something wrong with wanting a relationship that is built on loyalty, love, trust, and self-control? I think not. I submit to you that women have become *so* out of control sexually because of a
lack of respect from the men/fathers/uncles/brothers in their lives. Women
have become so consumed with sexual satisfaction that they are, in increas-
ingly alarming numbers, succumbing to homosexuality and other degrading sexual acts.

I had a woman once tell me that I must have a "mental problem" to think
that my husband should be faithful to me. She said all men cheat—why should
my husband be any different? But I am convinced that what we are experiencing now comes from an absence of God's presence with us.

What my husband is afraid of is exposure. Exposing his deeds would cause
vulnerability, and he could not allow vulnerability—that's a sign of weakness.
Have you ever watched *Cheaters*? On this show, the victim in the relationship
starts the show by telling their side of the story and the background information on the person accused of cheating. Then the investigation of the daily
schedule of the person in question begins. A group of private investigators
follows the person around to see if they are secretly seeing someone else. The
private investigators secretly record the activities of the cheater and the one

that they are cheating with. Then the climax is that the cheater gets caught sleeping with the one that is the object of their obsession.

Every time, the cheater appears shocked and upset that the victim would go to such lengths to expose their activities. The guilt is not from the acts that they have committed but from the exposure of the acts on national TV.

Exposure is powerful. It leaves the cheater confused and uncertain about what to do next. Should I leave with the one I am cheating with or should I go with the one that has exposed my wrong deeds?

But God's exposure—or more accurately, God's correction—is given to provide direction and to bring us into a right relationship with Him. We confuse judgment with damnation. God's intention is to redeem us to Him. There can be no redemption without first bringing to light that there is a need to redeem. When God says "I judge you a sinner," He is saying, "I know that it is not in you alone to be holy—that is why I sent My Son!" In every generation prior to Jesus coming to earth, men proved that they were incapable of living without sin. That is the good news of the Gospel.

God showed me a glimpse of His plan. All of one particular day, my husband had been scheming—trying to find a reason to leave the house—and then, late that afternoon, a friend called, needing his help. So, now he had a plan—it wouldn't take him long to help his friend, and then he could spend the evening with his new friend. After four hours, I hadn't heard from him. I started to call him, and God said, "Don't call." So, I didn't, but my stomach was in knots. There was that same old feeling again—the feeling of betrayal. I continued working, praying, and crying. He was up to his old tricks, and our anniversary was the next day. My heart was churning and gripped with fear.

Seven hours passed. I heard the car pull into the driveway, and I dried my tears. I told myself, "Get it together...show no emotion...suppress your hurt and pain for now....allow God to work." So, I continued to work. Michael came into the house, but he didn't come to find me as he usually does. He went to the bedroom, then to the bathroom, and he washed himself and changed clothes. He spoke to each of our children and went back to our bedroom. God said, "Don't move…"

I decided to slip into bed for a few hours, and as I got in bed, I could smell her on his breath, and I felt sick to my stomach.

Now, the end of the story is greater than the beginning. Michael had been out all night with another woman and came in smelling of her. In my heart, I knew he had chosen to be with another "babe." I had been feeling this way all summer long as I saw him leave the room to talk on the phone, or not answer the phone for no apparent reason while the person kept calling back again and again. My heart was racing—will I get hurt again? I didn't want to hurt anymore, so I got angry instead. Now I was fuming.

Then God said, "Don't say anything." So I didn't. I didn't move, and I didn't say anything. I worked way into the wee hours of the morning until I couldn't bear to keep my eyes open any longer. I decided to slip into bed for a few hours, and as I got in bed, I could smell her on his breath, and I felt sick to my stomach. I could smell her cheap cologne, so I moved to get up out of bed. "I can't sleep with this." God said, "Get back in bed," so I did, and surprisingly, I fell asleep very quickly, only to wake up an hour later. Then the Spirit of God spoke these words to me:

I know how you feel, but I want you to endure this so that you understand the depth of My love. I know you're hurting—this is a pain worse than death. But you can't fully write about what you don't feel. For more years than I care to think about, I have gotten into bed with My Bride, and she is wreaking with the scent of her lovers to the point of making Me sick with nausea. She loves on her other gods without a thought of what she's doing to

Me. But I get in bed with her *willingly* because I AM committed to her. Yes, she makes me sick to my stomach, but I still love her.

My death on the cross wasn't just for her to *accept* Me as her personal Savior, but it was for Me, too. I *chose* the cross because I *chose* her, knowing that she would turn her back on Me and follow other gods. On the cross, I *chose* in advance to *forgive* her and not change My mind about My commitment to saving her. She's *still* My Bride, and even if she leaves Me, I will go to look and then find her to bring her home again. On the cross, I *chose* to *love* her, in sickness and in health, for better or for worse—*until death do us unite*, because *death* is what brought us together.

And I *chose you*, Lauraine, to endure this suffering so that you would tell not just your children but the world what it feels like to be betrayed—not just once but over and over and over again— but never leave…

Daughter, you live in a time when people give up before the marriage begins because no one wants to be with an unfaithful lover. *Neither do I*! But, My message to you is still the same—I *chose* her, and I'll choose her over and over and over again because I won't go back on My word. From the beginning of time, I *chose* the cross even though I *saw in advance* all of her mistakes, her lies, and her secrets. You see, the cross wasn't just for you—it was for Me, too. Just as I display the rainbow as evidence of My covenant with man to never bring a flood again to destroy the world, so the cross displays and demonstrates My *commitment* to *forgive* those that *accept* Me as their Savior. This is *My love story*, with a bittersweet passage, and it is time for My people to come back to Me with a new and fresh look at who I AM. I want *My people* to look at My face and see My tears streaming down My cheeks, feel My pain and anguish—the heaviness in My heart as I choke back the years of tears that I have cried.

I woke up very early one morning, weeping uncontrollably. I felt the prompting of the Holy Spirit to weep and wail prophetically. The Holy Spirit began to reveal to me that my husband was struggling with being faithful to me. He showed me in a vision that my husband was seeing someone at work. Holy Spirit revealed her name, address, and so many other details. My husband denied all of it. He profusely denied any unfaithfulness. But this was wrong on my part—this was not the Holy Spirit's intent in revealing this to me. Instead, Holy Spirit wanted me to intercede.

One Sunday morning, after two weeks of weeping each morning and the revelation of my husband's struggles, with ever-increasing intensity in my personal experiences to heighten my passion for prophetically weeping, the Holy Spirit woke me and told me to go to the kitchen table. On the kitchen table was a Bible. I opened it to Hosea, and I began to read from Hosea, beginning at the first chapter. As stated in a previous chapter, I had become very familiar with the book of Hosea, but the Holy Spirit had *new revelation* for me.

Hosea starts out like this (Hosea 1–2 MSG):

> *This is God's Message to Hosea son of Beeri. It came to him during the royal reigns of Judah's kings Uzziah, Jotham, Ahaz, and Hezekiah. This was also the time that Jeroboam son of Joash was king over Israel.*
>
> *The first time GOD spoke to Hosea He said:*
>
> > *"Find a whore and marry her. Make this whore the mother of your children. And here's why: This whole country has become a whorehouse, unfaithful to Me, GOD."*
>
> *Hosea did it. He picked Gomer daughter of Diblaim. She got pregnant and gave him a son.*
>
> *Then GOD told him:*

"Name him Jezreel. It won't be long now before I'll make the people of Israel pay for the massacre at Jezreel. I'm calling it quits on the kingdom of Israel. Payday is coming! I'm going to chop Israel's bows and arrows into kindling in the valley of Jezreel."

Gomer got pregnant again. This time she had a daughter. GOD told Hosea:

"Name this one No-Mercy. I'm fed up with Israel. I've run out of mercy. There's no more forgiveness. Judah's another story. I'll continue having mercy on them. I'll save them. It will be their GOD who saves them, not their armaments and armies, not their horsepower and manpower."

After Gomer had weaned No-Mercy, she got pregnant yet again and had a son. GOD said:

"Name him Nobody. You've become nobodies to Me, and I, GOD, am a nobody to you.

"But down the road the population of Israel is going to explode past counting, like sand on the ocean beaches. In the very place where they were once named Nobody, they will be named God's Somebody. Everybody in Judah and everybody in Israel will be assembled as one people. They'll choose a single leader. There'll be no stopping them— a great day in Jezreel!

"Rename your brothers 'God's Somebody.' Rename your sisters 'All Mercy.'

"Haul your mother into court. Accuse her! She's no longer My wife. I'm no longer her husband. Tell her to quit dressing like a whore, displaying her breasts for sale. If she refuses, I'll rip off her clothes and expose her, naked as a newborn. I'll turn her skin into dried-out leather, her body into a badlands landscape, a rack of bones in the desert. I'll have nothing to do with her children, born one and all in a whorehouse.

Face it: Your mother's been a whore, bringing bastard children into the world. She said, 'I'm off to see my lovers! They'll wine and dine me, dress and caress me, perfume and adorn me!' But I'll fix her: I'll dump her in a field of thistles, then lose her in a dead-end alley. She'll go on the hunt for her lovers but not bring down a single one. She'll look high and low but won't find a one. Then she'll say, 'I'm going back to my husband, the one I started out with. That was a better life by far than this one.' She didn't know that it was I all along who wined and dined and adorned her, that I was the one who dressed her up in the big-city fashions and jewelry that she wasted on wild Baal-orgies. I'm about to bring her up short: No more wining and dining! Silk lingerie and gowns are a thing of the past. I'll expose her genitals to the public. All her fly-by-night lovers will be helpless to help her. Party time is over. I'm calling a halt to the whole business, her wild weekends and unholy holidays. I'll wreck her sumptuous gardens and ornamental fountains, of which she bragged, 'Whoring paid for all this!' They will soon be dumping grounds for garbage, feeding grounds for stray dogs and cats. I'll make her pay for her indulgence in promiscuous religion—all that sensuous Baal worship and all the promiscuous sex that went with it, stalking her lovers, dressed to kill, and not a thought for Me."

Then I heard the Spirit of God say:

You are not the only one that is *jealous*. I AM a jealous God. You are weeping prophetically because I weep for My Bride, the Church. Just as your husband gives you lip service of his adoring love but his heart seems far from you, I, too, have a Bride that worships Me on Sundays, but Sunday afternoon and all week long, their heart is far from Me. They have been taught to have an "experience" with Me— but they never *experience Me*. They want momentary gratification without the ties of a relationship. In a marriage, there is *covenant* and *commitment*. There is a point of submission of "my will" for the good of "our will" in a marriage. But, they want Me to submit to their will. They have the audacity to treat Me like a *sugar daddy*. As if I AM their puppet on a string. Don't they know who I AM?

My relationship with My Bride *today* is similar to a husband who is married to a woman who is unfaithful *but she won't leave him*. She won't leave his security, but she won't be faithful to him either. The leaders of My Church teach them to *worship* and *tithe*, but there is no mention of holiness—just a whole lot of lip service. I AM longing for more than a worship experience—I want a *relationship* with My Bride! I don't want *sex* without a marriage-covenant relationship. I want My Bride to know that she means more to Me than that. As she walks and talks with Me, she will know My *heart*, and she will submit to Me and *only Me*. She will not go whoring after other gods. She won't worship mere mortals— men that have elevated themselves to be little gods. I AM sickened when My day of worship is spent worshipping men. And they call themselves shepherds after My heart!

I have been reduced to nothing more than a sugar daddy? "If you tithe, He will send showers of blessings," they say, but tithing should be in response to their *changed* lives. One does not work without the other. Tithing only releases an open heaven once your life is surrendered and committed to *holiness*. Yes, tithing is a universal principle, but I want My Bride to have more than a sugar-daddy experience with Me. Holiness brings you into the place of *My glory*, and *My glory* brings you into a wealthy place, but I *choose* who will be made *rich*.

Then the Spirit of God said to go back to the text. And I read this:

GOD indicts the whole population: "No one is faithful. No one loves.
No one knows the first thing about God. All this cussing and lying and
killing, theft and loose sex, sheer anarchy, one murder after another!
And because of all this, the very land itself weeps and everything in it
is grief-stricken—animals in the fields and birds on the wing, even
the fish in the sea are listless, lifeless."2

I then heard the Spirit of God say:

Because I have taken so much from you, I have removed My hand
from you. This is causing havoc in your land. There is corruption
on every side. But, I AM bringing down every high thing that is
exalted above Me. And you will know that I AM God. The rest-
lessness—that's Me! The uncertainty—that's Me! I AM bringing
correction where there was lawlessness. Corruption has even infil-
trated your food and water supplies. Now you want your children to
return to Me—because you can no longer do anything with them.
I AM no puppet on a string. Even many prophets have given you
easy words to entice you, but I send the prophets to bring correction and order in times of disobedience and lawlessness.

I then went back to Hosea 4 and 5, and they read:

But don't look for someone to blame. No finger pointing! You, priest,
are the one in the dock. You stumble around in broad daylight, and
then the prophets take over and stumble all night. Your mother is as
bad as you. My people are ruined because they don't know what's right
or true. Because you've turned your back on knowledge, I've turned
My back on you priests. Because you refuse to recognize the revelation
of God, I'm no longer recognizing your children. The more priests, the

---

2. Hosea 4:1–3 MSG.

more sin. They traded in their glory for shame. They pig out on My people's sins. They can't wait for the latest in evil. The result: You can't tell the people from the priests, the priests from the people. I'm on My way to make them both pay and take the consequences of the bad lives they've lived. They'll eat and be as hungry as ever, have sex and get no satisfaction. They walked out on Me, their GOD, for a life of rutting with whores.

Wine and whiskey leave My people in a stupor. They ask questions of a dead tree, expect answers from a sturdy walking stick. Drunk on sex, they can't find their way home. They've replaced their God with their genitals. They worship on the tops of mountains, make a picnic out of religion. Under the oaks and elms on the hills they stretch out and take it easy. Before you know it, your daughters are whores and the wives of your sons are sleeping around. But I'm not going after your whoring daughters or the adulterous wives of your sons. It's the men who pick up the whores that I'm after, the men who worship at the holy whorehouses—a stupid people, ruined by whores!

You've ruined your own life, Israel—but don't drag Judah down with you! Don't go to the sex shrine at Gilgal, don't go to that sin city Bethel, don't go around saying "GOD bless you" and not mean it, taking God's name in vain. Israel is stubborn as a mule. How can GOD lead him like a lamb to open pasture? Ephraim is addicted to idols. Let him go. When the beer runs out, it's sex, sex, and more sex. Bold and sordid debauchery—how they love it! The whirlwind has them in its clutches. Their sex-worship leaves them finally impotent.

Listen to this, priests! Attention, people of Israel! Royal family—all ears! You're in charge of justice around here. But what have you done? Exploited people at Mizpah, ripped them off on Tabor, victimized them at Shittim. I'm going to punish the lot of you.

I know you, Ephraim, inside and out. Yes, Israel, I see right through you! Ephraim, you've played your sex-and-religion games long enough. All Israel is thoroughly polluted. They couldn't turn to God if they wanted to. Their evil life is a bad habit. Every breath they take is a whore's breath. They wouldn't recognize GOD if they saw Me.

Bloated by arrogance, big as a house, they're a public disgrace, the lot of them—Israel, Ephraim, Judah—lurching and weaving down their guilty streets. When they decide to get their lives together and go off looking for GOD once again, they'll find it's too late. I, GOD, will be long gone. They've played fast and loose with Me for too long, filling the country with their bastard offspring. A plague of locusts will devastate their violated land.

Blow the ram's horn shofar in Gibeah, the bugle in Ramah! Signal the invasion of Sin City! Scare the daylights out of Benjamin! Ephraim will be left wasted, a lifeless moonscape. I'm telling it straight, the unvarnished truth, to the tribes of Israel.

Israel's rulers are crooks and thieves, cheating the people of their land, and I'm angry, good and angry. Every inch of their bodies is going to feel My anger.

Brutal Ephraim is himself brutalized—a taste of his own medicine! He was so determined to do it his own worthless way. Therefore I'm pus to Ephraim, dry rot in the house of Judah.

When Ephraim saw he was sick and Judah saw his pus-filled sores, Ephraim went running to Assyria, went for help to the big king. But he can't heal you. He can't cure your oozing sores.

I'm a grizzly charging Ephraim, a grizzly with cubs charging Judah. I'll rip them to pieces—yes, I will! No one can stop Me now. I'll drag them off. No one can help them. Then I'll go back to where I came from until they come to their senses. When they finally hit rock bottom, maybe they'll come looking for Me.

After reading this, my weeping intensified. I was trembling at the thought of these words. They had meaning for *right then* in that moment. God's message was loud and clear. Then I heard the Spirit say:

"Don't play with My emotions," says the Spirit of God. "You say and do what you think I want you to say and do. I AM not impressed by your outward show of affection by your worship of Me, for I see you when you don't realize I AM there. I see you in your private meetings. I see you loving other gods, elevating them and whoring yourself with them. I AM *a jealous God!* You will have *no other* gods before Me. I AM tired of loving you and you won't love Me in return. I AM God, but I feel *empty* without your affection being given to Me *only.*

"I AM causing all of creation to cry out in response to your repulsive behaviors. I AM causing unusual season changes, natural disasters—even that you would be turned to your own reprobate mind, feeding your lustful and degrading desires. I AM allowing you to feed your ugly flesh with your lustful ways. Homosexuality, drug abuse, heightened adultery, cheating, deception—and it starts with those that call themselves My shepherds. Their hearts are *so* far from Me.

"You keep saying that the enemy has stolen some things from you. The enemy did not steal them—I took them! I removed My hand from you because of your disobedience and lack of reverence for Me. I don't *need* your lip service. I need your *reverence.*

"I AM repulsed by you. Do you not see what you are doing to Me? I deserve your faithfulness. I have done nothing but love you, provide for you, protect you. But as soon as you leave My *presence*, you forget Me.

"Why can't you love Me as a faithful Bride should? Don't keep using the excuse of how you were done wrong by others. It's time for you to take responsibility for your own actions.

"I knew that when I took away your *finances* and your *resources*, you would go looking for another source. Just not Me! You looked to the pope *privately*. In *secret* you kissed his ring. You *bowed down* to him as if he really *is Christ*. I AM *releasing My judgment* on those who lie prostrate to other gods!

"Although you *bow*, I still have an army that will not bow to another. There's a *quick spiritual* changing of the guard taking place. My intercessors have been crying out for years on your behalf—that you would have a change of heart, but you refused. You went from bad to worse. I knew you would. That's why My *elect* have been lying in wait. Just like David had to hide in caves until Saul died, it is again My *elect* that are waiting. As a mother waiting to deliver her baby, so it is now. And this birth is with much pain. Out of dark places, they are *rising up*. Many of them don't even go to a church, but they are *Mine*.

"I cry for you. I ache for you because I must punish you for what you have done to Me. Did you really think that I would let you act this way indefinitely and still stay by your side—loving and caring for you? Your days are coming to an end!

"It *scares* Me that you can be so careless and reckless in spite of all My warnings. The more I warn you, the more reckless you become. You serve Me with your lips and your words, but I *feel no love coming from you*—especially My shepherds. Is this what I *called* you from the world for? To mock Me? I have sheep that are lost and wandering in dangerous territory and *will not* come back because of you, shepherds. You won't even go after My sheep when they have been abused—either by you, other sheep, by wolves disguised as sheep, or by the goats that you have allowed to come in and mix with the sheep. You are so caught up in feeding your flesh that you don't see the sheep that you have caused to go astray.

"But I AM the *Good Shepherd.* I will not have My sheep unattended and scattered. I AM raising up shepherds that have *My heart*— that will obey *My voice*—that will seek after Me, that will establish works because they heard Me calling them.

"It's a *new day*, and I AM creating a *new way* out of this wilderness. You will not drive *My sheep* any longer. I *will* cause calamity to come. I *will* strip you of everything that you hold dear. *Your kingdom* is coming down. Didn't you read in My Word—you will *have no other* gods before Me?"

After hearing these things from the Spirit of God, there was so much fear in my heart. I asked God, "What do You want me to do with this, Lord?" Then the Spirit of God said, "Write these things down." This is how the process of writing this book began.

Then the Spirit asked me, "Who is your God, Lauraine—whom or what do you worship?" My first response was, "God the Father, of course!" But the Spirit asked the question again, and I was silenced. It took three days of real soul-searching and reckoning with who I had become to answer this question. Looking at my life and where I was at that point, I realized that my work and building a business had consumed my every waking moment. I put work ahead of my family, and all of my priorities were misplaced. And trust me—I attended worship every week and I was a tither, but God was not first.

Idol worship? What are idols? In Exodus 20:4–6 (NASB), it states:

You shall not make for yourself an idol, or any likeness of what is in
heaven above or on the earth beneath or in the water under the earth.
You shall not worship them or serve them; for I, the LORD your God,
am a jealous God, visiting the iniquity of the fathers on the children,
on the third and the fourth generations of those who hate Me, but
showing lovingkindness to thousands, to those who love Me and keep
My commandments.

Webster's Dictionary defines an *idol* as "a representation or symbol of an object of worship"; "a false god"; "a form or appearance visible but without substance"; or "an object of extreme devotion." What I have come to understand is that idol worship is not limited to worship of a statue, picture in a frame, or object. This notion of idol worship extends itself to other created things and human beings as well. It is the belief that there is something or someone that we hold to be more important or in higher esteem than God.

But how did idol worship begin? What is its origin? As a bit of a Biblical history lesson, we will begin with Noah and the ark. I find it amazing that God used Noah and his descendants to replenish the earth after the flood. At the age of 480, Noah (despite the ridicule of his peers) threw caution to the wind and trusted God by building the ark and preaching repentance for one hundred twenty years. The reason God brought judgment on the earth was because human beings had become so wicked and even their thoughts were constantly evil. Therefore, God repented that He had made man. In Genesis 6:7 (NASB), God said, "I will blot out man whom I have created from the face of the land, from man to animals to creeping things and to birds of the sky; for I am sorry that I have made them."

So, God used Noah to replenish and purify the earth, and within his lifetime, the human race returned to its wickedness and *idolatry*.

The first mention of idol worshippers is in Joshua 24:2, where Joshua mentions to the children of Israel that Abraham's father and grandfather—Terah and Nahor—worshipped other gods. Why would God choose Abraham (who was called Abram at the time), seeing that his father, grandfather, and great-grandfather worshipped idols? Why is it that Abraham would choose to travel a different path than his forefathers?

I believe that Abraham's response to this question would be that he heard the audible voice of God, and as he obeyed that voice, his life got better—so much so that everyone around him took notice. I believe that even his family members could see changes in Abraham, his wealth, and favor and wanted to know why he got all of the breaks. They wanted to know how he was able to choose the better path above everyone else. Even his nephew knew that favor was found in walking with him and not against him. That's why when his own father died, Lot held on to Uncle Abraham as father because of the favor associated with him.

Most people, especially Christians, when asked if they participate in idol worship, would say no. But upon further investigation, you would find that they do practice some form of idol worship.

When I began to search my own heart concerning spiritual matters, I realized that I had expected God to play second fiddle to other things and people. My god had become money, perceived power—which were nothing in the grand scheme of things—and people that were not worthy of the pedestal that I had placed them on—specifically, religious leaders of our time. I worshipped pastors, prophets, apostles, and anyone else that had gifts from God. I was in awe of their positions and power. Through my actions, I treated them as *equal* with God. God brought me to a place of brokenness and repentance by exposing the things that I was worshipping. I was taken to the Scripture in Deuteronomy 29:9–29, which deals with God's covenant with the children of Israel regarding idol worship. It reads:

> *Carefully follow the terms of this covenant, so that you may prosper in everything you do. All of you are standing today in the presence of the LORD your God—your leaders and chief men, your elders and officials, and all the other men of Israel, together with your children and your*

*wives, and the foreigners living in your camps who chop your wood
and carry your water. You are standing here in order to enter into a
covenant with the L*ORD *your God, a covenant the L*ORD *is making
with you this day and sealing with an oath, to confirm you this day
as His people, that He may be your God as He promised you and as
He swore to your fathers, Abraham, Isaac and Jacob. I am making
this covenant, with its oath, not only with you who are standing here
with us today in the presence of the L*ORD *our God but also with those
who are not here today.*

*You yourselves know how we lived in Egypt and how we passed through
the countries on the way here. You saw among them their detestable
images and idols of wood and stone, of silver and gold. Make sure
there is no man or woman, clan or tribe among you today whose
heart turns away from the L*ORD *our God to go and worship the gods
of those nations; make sure there is no root among you that produces
such bitter poison.*

*When such a person hears the words of this oath and they invoke a
blessing on themselves, thinking, "I will be safe, even though I persist
in going my own way," they will bring disaster on the watered land
as well as the dry. The L*ORD *will never be willing to forgive them;
His wrath and zeal will burn against them. All the curses written in
this book will fall on them, and the L*ORD *will blot out their names
from under heaven. The L*ORD *will single them out from all the tribes
of Israel for disaster, according to all the curses of the covenant written in this Book of the Law.*

*Your children who follow you in later generations and foreigners who
come from distant lands will see the calamities that have fallen on the
land and the diseases with which the L*ORD *has afflicted it. The whole
land will be a burning waste of salt and sulfur—nothing planted,
nothing sprouting, no vegetation growing on it. It will be like the*

destruction of Sodom and Gomorrah, Admah and Zeboyim, which the LORD *overthrew in fierce anger. All the nations will ask: "Why has the* LORD *done this to this land? Why this fierce, burning anger?"*

And the answer will be: "It is because this people abandoned the covenant of the LORD, *the God of their ancestors, the covenant He made with them when He brought them out of Egypt. They went off and worshiped other gods and bowed down to them, gods they did not know, gods He had not given them. Therefore the* LORD's *anger burned against this land, so that He brought on it all the curses written in this book. In furious anger and in great wrath the* LORD *uprooted them from their land and thrust them into another land, as it is now."*

The secret things belong to the LORD *our God, but the things revealed belong to us and to our children forever, that we may follow all the words of this law.*

This encounter moved me, and I needed more direction as to where God was leading His Church. There was a greater plan, and I knew that God would reveal it...in His own time...in His own way.

6

I CHOOSE TO LIVE

Learn from yesterday, live for today, hope for tomorrow.

ALBERT EINSTEIN

E very day, starting from the day that we had lunch with Bishop Powers in early 2008, Michael received a call from him. It was as if where one bishop stopped, the other took up the torch to give direction and guidance to Michael and me. But God had plans through this relationship...

We've met many anointed people, but none quite like Bishop Powers. He was exceptional and unforgettable, to say the least. For everyone that we encountered in the five years that we spent with him daily, God would give him insight into their lives, and Bishop Powers would pour life into them by giving them direction and hope for the future. Everything that he imparted was accurate, precise, and timely.

Right after my meeting with Bishop Powers, there was a change in his living arrangements, and we picked him up to move him into one of the local hotels near our home. We were able to negotiate a great weekly rate for him, and it was around the corner from where we lived. The best part about these arrangements was that we got to spend quality time with him every day. At the same moment in time that our businesses went belly up, time with Bishop Powers filled our days where business activities used to consume them.

Bishop Powers completed over sixty years in ministry. He began his ministry at age thirteen, but he was told that he first heard God's voice when he was only three years old. He told us that his mother had been Catholic and used to go to a Pentecostal Church on Sunday nights to tease those that would become slain in the Spirit. But on one particular Sunday evening, as she was preparing to tease others, she became slain in the Spirit herself. Not long after hearing God's voice, Bishop Powers's mother became ill. As a toddler, he prayed for his mother's healing, and she was healed in that moment. This began a supernatural journey for both him and his mother and a legacy of miracles that followed his life.

Bishop, or Apostle Powers, as he was also known—was called the Boy Wonder Preacher because of his anointing, and as a young boy, he was the first to preach on television soon after its invention in the 1940s. He was also the youngest boy preacher on a regular radio program in New York City. At seventeen years old, Bishop Powers was the substitute pastor for one of the largest churches in Harlem.

In June 1955, Bishop Powers married the late Mary Wilson, and to their union were born four daughters. Unfortunately, I never got the opportunity to meet Pastor Mary Powers, but I heard so many wonderful things about her. Bishop Powers mentioned to us that one night back in the early '70s, while they were asleep, the Spirit of God shook their bed. When he woke up, the Spirit told him that he was to make his wife, Mary, the pastor of the church in Atlanta, and from that day on, she became pastor. It was unheard of—especially in the Bible-belt South—that a woman would become a pastor of a church.

Amazingly, he blamed himself for his wife's untimely death because he wasn't there. He was in New York, and she was in Atlanta. They spoke that morning, and she complained about feeling like someone had taken a needle and was poking her insides. He asked if she wanted him to come home to Atlanta right away, but she told him not to make a special trip, but he received a call later that evening informing him that she had gone into a coma. She never came to and later transitioned from this life to the next.

Doing ministry was Bishop Powers's number-one priority—not family. When anyone called him to minister, he would drop everything to go. Even family special days such as birthdays, holidays, and graduations played second fiddle to the opportunity to minister. Therefore, his relationships with his children suffered, but his wife and mother were the glue that kept the family together, giving him the opportunity to soar in ministry. They shared an exceptional life together and accomplished impossible things because of their love and commitment to each other and to doing ministry.

They both were committed. He could *not* do ministry at the level that he did ministry without his wife's vow to play her part in making family and ministry work successfully. His wife and mother appeared to be best friends— they did everything together. They raised the children and grandchildren together. They planned vacations together. They even transitioned from this life within months of each other.

We looked forward to our meal times with Bishop Powers because he had so many stories to tell of his time in ministry. My mother-in-law would prepare dinner and dessert, and we would sit for hours after dinner listening to his faith-filled stories of how God supernaturally saw him through every situation that he faced.

He spoke of the time when he was headed to the airport en route to Africa on a mission trip, when a church that he oversaw called to tell him that they could not meet their monthly obligations and were about to be foreclosed on. They needed five thousand dollars, which was exactly what he had for his trip. He was going to purchase plane tickets once he got to the airport, but instead, he dropped by that church to deliver the five thousand dollars to the pastor.

Most people would have headed home after that, but not Bishop Powers. After leaving the church building, he drove on to the airport and said, "I know God will provide!" Once at the airport, he got in line at the ticket counter— that was *faith* in action. Then a woman came over to him and told him that God told her to give him five thousand dollars, and she wrote out the check to him while he was standing in line.

There were so many stories like this one where God always showed Himself strong and mighty for Bishop Powers. And usually, it involved God showing

Bishop Powers something that had happened or was going to happen to an individual, and that individual would turn out to be someone who wanted to bless him in return for his anointing.

Every day that we spent with Bishop Powers was an adventure. We met so many affluent people—politicians, pro athletes, business owners, inventors, etc. Each one that we encountered, after receiving a word of direction, would be moved to do extraordinary things for Bishop Powers.

What we learned is that early in Bishop Powers's ministry, he had become very wealthy. But because of the compassion that he had for others, he gave so much away. He didn't plan properly for his later years so that he would not be obligated to continue to minister daily—this was a time when he should have been more of a mentor to young pastors. Living with concern for his means of income should not have consumed his time. But his oldest daughter lovingly cared for him financially, so that he didn't have to worry and could live comfortably.

In evaluating our time spent with Bishop Powers, it is obvious now that God was honing our spiritual skills by our association with him. There was no hocus-pocus or anything like that. But it was further development through daily experience with his anointing and watching him as he ministered. It was not for us to be amazed by his gift as others were. Rather, we participated with his ministry, along with his grandson by marriage, Dr. Amos Boyd.

Bishop Powers was well equipped for training and developing church leaders. He had done this his entire ministry of sixty years. He named pastor after pastor that he had trained, but also Bishop Powers helped them establish their local churches. We were no different, except that we had, during the bulk of 2008–2010, one-on-one time with him every day.

But more than just the regular training, Bishop Powers warned us about what ministry can do to a family. That ministry takes on a life of its own if you allow it to. Hindsight is usually 20/20, and Bishop Powers had the benefit of seeing the effects of some of his decisions, and he infused this into his training with us.

It was more than just training. He gave us impartation. Here he was near the end of his life, with no church to lead (he had given his church to his daughter and son-in-law after the death of his wife), and he wanted to impart himself to us. This speaks to the character of the man. He followed God at all costs.

And it cost him a lot. After his wife died, his life became scattered because not only was she the glue that kept the household together, but she was a source of strength for him. He kind of lost his way. Therefore, many of his final years were spent trying to recapture his early years of ministry and miracles. But because of the economy and all that was happening in the world, most people had grown cold toward church.

That's why he was so happy helping us—because we hung on to his every word. He told us about all of the great ministry leaders that he got a chance to meet and to minister with. Some of the people were Mother Rosa Horn, out of Brooklyn, New York; Aimee Semple McPherson; A. A. Allen; Kathryn Kuhlman; Billy Graham, just to name a few. He even mentioned some that did not line up with how he preferred to do ministry because of their flamboyant flare—Sweet Daddy Grace, Father Divine, and Reverend Ike—all out of New York City. Although he knew much about the character of some of these ministry leaders, he did not place judgment on them. He accepted each on their own meritorious acts.

During this time, we cared for Bishop Powers's needs. My husband would shave him, iron his clothes, and tie all of his ties so he wouldn't have to, and I became his personal assistant. We encouraged him to write a book about his ministry, but he never got around to completing it. But we did help put the sparkle back in his eyes. We were able to help him reconnect with old friends that he had ministered to and with in years past, such as Demond Wilson, from the *Sanford and Son* television show, and the jeweler that made all of Elvis Presley's jewelry. We were also able to find addresses, phone numbers, and email addresses of old friends, colleagues in ministry, and members of his church, and we created a monthly newsletter to keep them informed of where he was ministering each month.

He dedicated those final years to helping us to establish a church. On October 19, 2008, Bishop Milton Powers ordained my husband and me as pastors of the Branch of Life Deliverance Church, which was affectionately called the BOLD Church. The ordination services were to start that day at five p.m., and all participants were to be in place by 4:30 p.m.

Everyone was there except for Bishop Powers and Dr. Boyd. By five p.m., the house was packed, but still there were no signs of Bishop Powers. My husband called to find out if everything was okay. Bishop Powers said that everything was okay and that they were on their way, but he didn't sound like himself.

So, at five p.m., we began the praise and worship. This would normally take at the most twenty to twenty-five minutes. We ended up having praise and worship for over an hour, waiting in anticipation for Bishop Powers's arrival—but still no show. My husband was embarrassed, so I went out to the audience and began delivering a message that neither one of us was prepared to deliver. Instead of telling them that Bishop Powers was not going to make it and that we would have to postpone the ordination, I decided to deliver a message of how God had called us into ministry. After the message, God moved, and I gave a word to a woman that was actually a visitor in the audience. Then we called for those that needed prayer for any concerns. While praying for those that had come up for a number of needs, Bishop Powers and Dr. Boyd walked in.

Looking flustered, Bishop Powers made his way to the podium and gave his apologies. We knew that Bishop Powers did not like showing up late. There had to be an explanation for them being *this* tardy. But they never gave an explanation.

We forgave them for this, but it always resonated in our hearts. What would cause them to show up almost two hours late? To give little or no explanation for it would have been unacceptable—except it was Bishop Powers—the kindest heart that you ever wanted to meet.

We moved past this and on to building the church. We had seen enough of what we didn't want but still needed clarity as to creating bylaws, creeds, and mission and vision statements that spoke to the heart of where God was taking us. Most of the time, Bishop Powers and my husband worked to formulate the wording, and I was to take the notes. I didn't mind except that I had ideas as well. But we worked together—our threefold cord that wasn't easily broken—to establish the heart of the BOLD Church.

In establishing the BOLD Church, we worked in collaboration with Vision of Faith International Church, which was led by Pastor Boyd and his wife. Pastor Boyd's wife was Bishop Powers's granddaughter. We all hit it off immediately. Whenever they had a conference or a revival meeting, we were eager to assist in any way that we could, and that included attending as many nights as possible to support the work that they were doing in north Atlanta.

This was solely the Holy Spirit that moved on me to perform
that song. No magic, but it was majestic in nature.

This association between the BOLD Church and Vision of Faith Church was not limited to just what was going on at our facilities, but also included when any of us, including Bishop Powers, ministered somewhere else. We each attended in support of the others. We became family. We loved and wanted the best for each other, in spite of any obstacles. We were a fierce team: Bishop Powers's anointing, Pastor Boyd's teaching, Pastor Michael's motivation, and my singing. What an amazing time we had!

I remember the first time that Dr. Boyd witnessed me singing a song "of the Lord." It was right after he delivered his message, and Bishop was beginning to minister the prophetic to the congregation. Without planning or preparation, while the musicians played, I closed my eyes, getting lost in the music. I began to sing the song of the Lord, and he got so excited. After services were over, he said, "That was *awesome* what you did! We need to do this after every service!" What he didn't understand was that I didn't orchestrate this. This was solely the Holy Spirit that moved on me to perform that song. No magic, but it was majestic in nature.

He had become so used to planning out services that the Holy Spirit had no room to move. He was stunned at my response. Then he said, "Well then, pray before services that the Holy Spirit *does that again*—in every service!"

We all laughed that off, but it stayed in my heart, and I remembered the Spirit talking about being treated like "a puppet on a string." I don't *ever* want to take the Holy Spirit for granted. This was not a show—and certainly not *my* show. God was trying to reach His people because of the state that they were in. As His servant, I felt compelled to honor Him in *how* I ministered as well as *how well*.

As our individual churches grew, so did our friendship—specifically, between my husband and Dr. Boyd. They usually talked daily and shared ideas about growth principles to help motivate each other.

We invited Dr. Boyd and his wife to eat dinner with us often, but most times, Dr. Boyd would come alone with his armor bearer. During these times that he came by with his armor bearer, we would all sit either in our formal dining room or at our kitchen table, which easily accommodated six or more people. As we were sitting around the kitchen table talking, I noticed that Dr. Boyd's armor bearer would not sit down. I kept motioning to him that he was welcome to sit down with us, but he refused. Then Dr. Boyd turned to me and said, "Oh, he doesn't sit down while he's working for me."

My husband and I looked at each other, puzzled but well aware of what he meant by that statement. We had come out of this kind of ministry, where you were always working to serve your leaders—never the other way around. But it was Jesus, as His disciples were sitting at the table, that bowed down on His knees to wash the feet of His disciples. His determination was to teach by example—how to lead from your knees.

I believe Jesus said it best in Matthew 20:28: "The Son of Man did not come to be served, but to serve." How can you lead from a place you've never been before? How can you lead without serving? And if we are all brothers and sisters, shouldn't we all serve each other? This produces a type of circle of life, doesn't it? We all serve each other; therefore, everyone is served.

But just as the British Royal Guard does not look at you while on post, neither did this gentleman. In my heart, I wanted to apologize to him for such bad behavior, but I knew if I said it out loud, I would bring more attention to this situation than I needed to at the time. They finally agreed to allow him to sit in our family room instead of standing guard while we were relaxing. I took this opportunity to go into our family room and sit with and talk to him. He was a very kind and gentle man with a wife, and at the time, two beautiful daughters and one on the way. I also learned that he was Dr. Boyd's first cousin. They grew up in Buffalo, New York, and Dr. Boyd was instrumental in his family moving to Georgia.

I could sense that his service to Dr. Boyd was in direct response to his gratitude for the difference that he made in his life, although Dr. Boyd was several years younger than he was.

Needless to say, the next time we visited Vision of Faith Church, I was interested in finding out more about this gentlemen and his family. When I met his wife, I hit it off with her immediately, as I did with most of the members at Vision of Faith Church—but she and their children were special. Their oldest daughter and I had one thing in common—we love handbags.

Another one of the members of Vision of Faith Church was Bishop Powers's grandson, Neil. When I met him, I heard the Spirit of God say, "Behold *your* son!" I went over to him and hugged his neck. He looked startled! I am sure he was thinking, "Who is this *crazy* woman hugging me?" At the time, I did not know that he was Bishop Powers's grandson—I only heard the Spirit telling me that he would be important to me, and I heard "*royal*." At the time, I didn't understand what this meant, but I knew it had to be important because his whole demeanor changed.

I found out that this is what his mother called him. She had died several years before I met him, and she, too, was very anointed. From that day on,

Neil began calling my husband and me Mom and Dad. He said that our family reminded him of Bishop Powers and his wife.

Soon afterwards, I found out that my husband was watching pornography, and because of our disagreement over the issues surrounding this, we asked Bishop Powers for counsel. Because Dr. Boyd was adjutant bishop to Bishop Powers, he became privy to this information.

Interestingly enough, Dr. Boyd invited us to one of their Wednesday-evening Bible studies immediately after this. Guess what the topic ended up being? You guessed right! Toward the end of his message, Dr. Boyd said, "My wife doesn't care if another woman is flirting with me. She knows that if another woman wants me, she better know that she's getting an entire family with four kids!"

After this, Dr. Boyd and my husband talked more than usual over the phone. Dr. Boyd seemed to get a whole lot of gratification out of the idea that we were having marital problems—almost as if he were gloating over it.

This infuriated me to no end. What kind of spiritual leader takes pleasure in other people's problems? Not one time did he encourage us to work out our differences. He took this opportunity to ridicule me for expecting faithfulness from my husband—he saw this as archaic.

From this point on, I limited my interaction with Dr. Boyd. This was tough because Bishop usually included him in everything that he did. For those times, I acquiesced and participated in silence. You know that this was hard for me to do because I am so outspoken. But I took this for the good of the team.

Soon after, we attended the Full Gospel Conference in downtown Atlanta. After the services that night, we all went to the Varsity to eat and fellowship. Of course, I wasn't so thrilled about that—but again, I acquiesced. Then it came up in conversation that a well-known pastor and his wife were going through a breakup due to him allegedly having a child by another woman.

Why did I subject myself to this nonsense? As I sat there, I knew that anyone that looked at me could see the fumes coming out of the top of my head.

Dr. Boyd then went on to ask the question of the group, "Which do you think would be better—for this pastor to go through this in their ministry when they have a large or a small congregation?" He continued, "I think it would be better if *my wife and I* went through this when we are small rather than when our congregation is large."

What? Was there trouble in paradise? That was the reason for him engaging our problems—it took the heat off of his own. He probably told his wife, "See, we're not the only ones having problems."

From that moment on, I stopped dwelling on my problems when I was around him, and I began to see things in a different light. Because of that, God was able to illuminate where He was trying to take me in understanding the reason for the relationship.

As God peeled back the layers, I became open to developing more of a relationship with Dr. Boyd's wife. Was this right or wrong? I don't know, but I felt that she needed a friend that was mature enough to not go around talking about her and her problems but could give friendly and godly advice on how to weather the storms of marriage. The only thing was, she was much more experienced in the ways of ministry than I was, and she took the approach of not talking about it at all. She prayed instead. It's always better to talk to God rather than human beings about your problems. God can guarantee the right outcome and give you peace while you wait on the expected ending. So, I started praying for her strength.

While we prayed, God revealed. My husband and I were invited to a friend's church in Duluth to hear Bishop Bloomer speak at a conference that they were sponsoring. When we arrived, we were expecting a large church building. Instead, it was a very small storefront church.

We came into the building and sat down near the door. My husband was skeptical. He felt that there was no way that Bishop Bloomer was going to speak at such a small church.

The pastor, who was our friend, did the welcome and then left the building to pick up Bishop Bloomer from the airport. They began praise and worship while the pastor left. About an hour to an hour and a half later, the pastor and Bishop Bloomer walked in. There were approximately twenty to twenty-five people in attendance.

Then Bishop Bloomer began his message: "What do you do when God has shut one door but hasn't opened another door?" We were intrigued. This was exactly what we had just gone through in our lives. God had shut the door for us at one church a few years prior, and it took a while for Him to open another door.

What we were amazed by was the fact that Bishop Bloomer, a world-renowned televangelist, would grace the threshold of a church this size. This was unheard of. Then Bishop Bloomer made the statement, "Small is the new *big*!" He had our full attention now.

This conversational message for the evening was much more intimate than we had ever experienced in a church setting, and we became so enthralled by it. It was only the first night of a week-long revival, and not many people attend revivals on a Monday night. We ended up attending every night and brought Bishop Powers the next night with us. Bishop Powers knew Bishop Bloomer from his association with Bishop T. D. Jakes.

Because of their association, Bishop Bloomer invited all of us to attend his Dominion 2011 Conference and Vantage Point—an exclusive meeting of pastors and leaders in the faith-based community. A part of this conference was dedicated to giving ideas to church leaders on how to generate other streams of income for the church so that it is not solely reliant on tithes and offerings. This included publishing books.

We received the email invitation on December 9, 2011, and the conference was to take place the first week in January 2012. As soon as I received the information, I registered my husband, myself, and Bishop Powers. When I spoke to Bishop Powers about the conference, he was excited. My husband decided that we would drive up the night before so that we didn't have to rush to get to where we were going and we could start out fresh in the morning.

A month went by, and on the week of the conference, Bishop Powers asked my husband if it would be okay if Dr. Boyd came along with us. This disturbed both my husband and me. Dr. Boyd had not paid the registration fees and had no intention of paying them. He just wanted to go along for the ride without contributing.

As my husband and I were discussing the issue, God placed in my spirit that Dr. Boyd was fleecing God's sheep at his congregation. Whoa! I told my husband what I heard, and he said he felt the same thing but just wasn't sure of it.

We just didn't know how to approach the subject with Bishop Powers because of their relationship. So, when my husband spoke to Bishop Powers about our decision, he was vague and just basically said that we preferred that he not ride with us.

Of course, Bishop Powers didn't take this lying down. He called me, thinking that he could convince me to help my husband change his mind. Little did he know that I was just as determined as—if not more determined than my husband was.

When he saw that I felt the same way that my husband felt, Bishop Powers asked me what the problem was with Dr. Boyd riding with us. I told him that it was disrespectful for him to go to this conference when we all had paid the registration fees, which were not cheap, and then take advantage of us by riding with us. He still didn't see anything wrong with this.

So, I laid it out for Bishop Powers. I told him what the Lord had shown me, and he didn't like it at all. In fact, he became defensive. He then told me that if Dr. Boyd wasn't invited, then he wouldn't go with us either. And he didn't!

Bishop Powers called one of the pastors in New York City that was scheduled to attend this same conference and told him what had happened between us. This pastor then offered to fly him in to the conference.

We all ended up arriving at the conference, and it appeared to be very difficult for Bishop Powers to deal with this new revelation. He was very standoffish with us, and I guess rightfully so under the circumstances. They say blood is thicker than water, right?

Other than this incident, the conference was well worth our attending. This conference afforded us the opportunity to speak with publishers regarding what it takes to publish a book. At the time that we attended this conference, I had only written less than ten thousand words. The publisher that we met with told us that with that amount of words, we would have "a great pamphlet." What a difference a year makes!

Once we were back at home, we saw less and less of Bishop Powers. Unfortunately for me, God gave me more revelations about Dr. Boyd that were terribly disturbing. Again, I confronted Bishop Powers about them, and he denied all of it.

One day, the wife of the gentleman that was Dr. Boyd's armor bearer came heavily into my spirit. So, I decided to call her. I said hello and that God had placed her on my heart. She began crying over the phone. She started confessing some things to me that only confirmed what the Spirit had already revealed to me and that my husband and I had asked Bishop Powers about.

I immediately hung up and called Bishop Powers, and I was ridiculed for listening to her. He told me that she was nothing more than a troublemaker, and that if I knew what was best for me, I wouldn't talk to her at all.

When I hung up the phone, I heard the Spirit say to me, "The spirit of Eli is present in this situation also." Oh, my God!

Now, months went by without any word from Bishop. My husband would call him faithfully every week and most times would get his voicemail. Bishop Powers usually answered his calls promptly.

On November 25, 2012, I received an email message from Bishop Jonathan Pierce with the Prophetic Campaign, inviting me to visit his Blog Talk Radio broadcast that night. The email stated that they didn't normally broadcast on Sunday nights, but God had given Bishop Pace a "right-now" urgent message for the Body of Christ. I didn't know why at the time, but I felt urgency about hearing this message.

The topic of the message was "FOCUS 36." He stated that this was a "season-sensitive word" for the Body of Christ and that God had shown him that the next thirty-six days that were remaining in that year were crucial—that we needed to shut down all of the distractions and fully focus on the direction that God was trying to take us. He was certain God was going to do in the next thirty-six days what we were not able to accomplish in the other 329 days that had already passed in the year of 2012.

He stated that strategic events and supernatural results would happen expeditiously within those thirty-six days. As we focused, God would give directions and instructions on how to proceed. He went on to state that our focus would give us 20/20 vision in the supernatural realm—20/20 vision for the things to come in the predicted spheres of our lives and the lives of those around us.

I knew in my spirit that this message was for me. I just didn't know what impact it would ultimately have on my life.

Every day, I woke up with expectancy. I got up—dressed up—prepared for something supernatural to happen. Little did I know that what was about to happen would blow our minds.

On New Year's Eve, my husband kept mentioning that he needed to call Bishop Powers. He finally called and spoke to him briefly, and Bishop stated that he was headed to a church near downtown Atlanta for watch-night services. We were having our own services, but Michael offered to pick him up to carry him to the church. He declined, saying that the church was sending someone over to get him. Funny thing…Bishop Powers did not allow Dr. Boyd to go with him on that night.

This is how God works—one of my husband's college friends was the one that picked up Bishop to carry him to the church. During the services, Bishop had a coughing spell, and the pastors suggested to my husband's friend to carry Bishop Powers to their office for him to get himself together. While in the pastor's office, Bishop struggled in his breathing and was holding his chest.

Then my husband's friend, who never left Bishop Powers's side during this ordeal, said that Bishop Powers began speaking in tongues with urgency, while sweating profusely. Then he said, "Boyd?" as if to ask God a question.

Then Bishop Powers was shaking his head, and again, he asked God the question, "Not Boyd?"

At this point, Bishop Powers's breathing became more of a strain as he had trouble gaining his positioning. As he was struggling to breathe, my husband's friend noticed that Bishop was sweating even more profusely than before and decided to go into the bathroom to get a wet towel to blot his brow. But when he came back into the room, Bishop Powers was on the floor, struggling for his life. At this point, he was no longer struggling in his breathing, but it was obvious that he was transitioning. He was hanging in the balance between mortal and immortal and having a conversation with the Lord regarding his grandson that he normally called Lamear but in this conversation he referred to as Boyd.

I CHOOSE TO FORGIVE

But they that wait upon the LORD shall renew their strength;
they shall mount up with wings as eagles; they shall run,
and not be weary; and they shall walk, and not faint.

ISAIAH 40:31 KJV

After Bishop Powers transitioned, Michael and I went through months of processing all that was recounted to us about the conversation between God and Bishop Powers in his final moments. We understood that God was teaching us the process of forgiveness. Forgiveness is not overlooking the deeds of those that transgress, but it is a pointedly confronting position that is taken first in order to give the opportunity for the transgressor to repent of their deeds. Without confrontation, most will not change their ways—they will just continue. But when confronted, the darkness is exposed to the light, and even a small glimmer of light can bring about the repentance needed to change the course of a person.

More than just confrontation, the death of this spiritual giant, Bishop Powers, caused a bigger community to hear and witness a portion of God's concerns—that those who lead God's people must lead with integrity and clean hands and not allow others to take advantage of God's people.

Through this twelve-year experience, God spoke of the need to restore His Church through the process of "tearing down the Asherah poles" that were erected in His house. Those idols that were made must fall down in the presence of Almighty God. The first law is that we must love the Lord our God with all of our heart, mind, soul, and strength, and there is no law more important.

During this twelve-year period of time, God instructed me to keep a journal of the things that were happening to and around us. Early on in this process, I didn't understand the magnitude of God's assignment for me. Although I kept a journal, I did not begin placing actual dates on my writing until 2014.

Yes…2014 was a hard year for me. In early February 2014, my mother received a diagnosis of pancreatic cancer, and on April 27, 2014, she transitioned from this life to eternity. One month later, my husband decided that I did not support him emotionally and did not allow him to be the man in our home. Therefore, he began staying away for days at a time to sort through what he wanted to do about our relationship.

Right after my mother's death, Holy Spirit showed me that my husband was going to have an affair with a co-worker. He told me her name and address and the issues of her marriage. At the time, I confronted my husband about it while walking a tightrope because I didn't want to make any more waves in our relationship than we already were experiencing.

After the death of my mother, my husband claimed that I did not make a point of including him in the planning of my mother's funeral. He made it clear that, in his perspective, my siblings and I went out of our way to exclude him from participation in the program and process.

It was a tough time, and I didn't realize that I had been so careless as to not include him in the plans and program. I was going through it, but I know that he had to have been going through it as well. It was insensitive of me to assume that it was *my* mother—not his—and that therefore, he had to consider me and all that I was going through and just suck it up.

Hindsight is 20/20, and I left the door wide open for the enemy to attack our marriage. I later found out that he took this other woman to Chastain Park on July 3, 2014, for the New Edition concert. I discovered this because he left the e-tickets in an envelope on his night stand. The next day, he came home, started a big fight with me, packed an overnight bag, and left. He blamed me for everything wrong with our marriage.

For days that turned into weeks and months, I felt that my world had totally fallen apart, and I couldn't handle it. I needed help, but no help could be found. Where was God *now*?

Then, on July 13, 14, and 15, 2014, each morning and night, I could smell the presence of angels. This was comforting because there were other times in the past twelve years when I had needed help and could smell this sweet fragrance, and I knew God had to have a plan for me.

Then, on July 16, the Spirit of God began to talk to me regarding His plan to make good on the promise that He'd made to bring restoration to me, beginning with my husband.

During this encounter, the Spirit of God showed me a vision of the other woman that my husband was having an affair with. The vision was of this woman riding in a car with a man that happened to be another co-worker that my husband despised. They were riding together to a place that my husband appeared to know and understand, and as they were driving off, my husband saw them. Once he saw this, it appeared that he fell apart.

At the time of this vision, this gentleman had not started working at the company yet. He didn't start until the following week, but in my vision on July 16, the Spirit of God called him by his last name.

Immediately after seeing this vision, God delivered His message of redemption and hope to me. God said that He was exposing and uncovering her secrets, her deception, and her betrayal, because she was going to betray my husband, and that this exposure would permanently break my husband's infatuation with her.

Then the Spirit of God told me:

> Stand *still* and see how I deliver you and perform that which I have promised you. Moses told the children of Israel, "Stand still and see the salvation of the Lord." But when did he tell them this? When

they were standing in front of the Red Sea, which appeared to be a dead end but was their *apparent salvation*. They were in between Pharaoh and his army and the Red Sea—between the bondage of their past and *the promise* of their future. My salvation *always* looks *impossible*. But what is *impossible* for man is *possible* with Me. So, I tell you that *today* you are standing at *your* Red Sea, and just as I delivered the children of Israel, I AM *delivering* you. I AM parting *your* Red Sea, and you will walk on *dry land*. Then I will cause your enemies to be swallowed up by the sea. Your Promised Land is on the other side of the sea. *Walk through* to the other side and receive your rest. I have seen your tears, your pain, your struggle to obey and follow Me, and I have also seen your faithfulness to obey Me—even when I told you how to *love* your husband. I know it hasn't been easy but it will be transforming…

Again, the Spirit of God said:

Stand *still* and see Me work this out for you. Is there *anything* too hard for Me? I will do it just as I promised you. Just as I have shown you. I know that the wicked appear to win, but it is all smoke and mirrors. It's not what it appears—*trust* Me! As these events unfold, you will understand.

These events will cause *transformation* in your husband, Michael. This is My doing. As you would turn off a running faucet, I AM turning off this running in his spirit. The running in his spirit represents what the enemy has used to bring about his destruction. He has used the sins of his forefathers—the enticement of lust, adultery, and fornication—to wreak havoc in your life. Your husband doesn't even know or understand what this is that is happening to and through him. Even when he wants to do the right thing, this spirit influences him to do the wrong thing. But I AM turning this off in him, just as easily as you would turn off a running faucet.

I AM restoring you. My daughter, you will recover *all*. I promised you, as I breathed on you with a new and fresh anointing in 2009—I told you that I AM *restoring you*, and that I AM beginning the restoration with your husband. I had to take you through the fire. I had to allow you to fight the spiritual lion, bear, and fox. Otherwise, you would not have the perfected anointing that you need to walk into your God-created destiny. You had to have your *faith* in Me built up so that you would *know* that there is *nothing too hard for Me* and that I have *chosen* you to be My servant. Your marriage had to *look* completely dead. It had to *look* like it was totally falling apart so that you and those around you would learn to trust Me. I AM *the resurrection and the life*. I resurrect that which is *dead* in your life so that you *know* that it was *only* possible through Me. No one else promised to restore you but Me, and no one else is *able* to. I AM *restoring you*. I gave you nine months living with your mother—not to hurt you but to give you *every day* with her for nine months to birth something *new* in you—even now. That which you have prophesied *is* coming to pass—even in this hour. And it will cause a *sudden, instantaneous, and swift change* in your husband and in your circumstances. This change in your husband and your circumstances will cause a chain reaction—a domino effect of sorts. All those promises that I made to you will begin to flow, and nothing and no one will ever be able to stop, slow down, or halt the *manifestation* of *all* that I *promised you*. Stay faithful, focused, and true to your calling. I AM is *always* with you.

The months that ensued were the hardest part of this transition from *who* I used to be to *who* I was to become. Every day for almost nine months after this, I felt a knot in my stomach and in my throat. I couldn't seem to shake these emotions from having just lost my mother and my husband. How do you grieve the dead and the living? Here I was, grieving my mother's death *and* the death of my marriage. Then it hit me. I dug out my journal and began reading and flipping back through the pages of writing that I'd done to capture all that I was experiencing, and there it was. Back in December of 2013, I had been awakened by a spirit (not sure who sent it) asking me, "Which would you prefer to lose, your mother or your husband?"

Back in December of 2013, I had been awakened by a spirit (not sure who sent it) asking me, "Which would you prefer to lose, your mother or your husband?"

Fast forward six months, and it appeared that I actually lost both. I couldn't believe that I was going through this. Most days, I just went through the motions, forgetting things that would normally be routine activities that came easily, but now it was a struggle completing them.

I couldn't seem to get rid of the anxiety and desperation. Why was I going through this? What did I do to deserve this? Why did God reveal so much about this woman and other details to me? Was this God or was this the enemy—or maybe it was just me wanting something horrible to happen in revenge for all that I had suffered. Whatever it was, I was in so much pain.

Why would God *cause* me to go through this on purpose? This seemed so unfair and undeserved. I was a good person. I wasn't perfect, but I worked hard to do the right things. I was a tither, and I did what I could to help those in need. So, why would I have to go through all of this?

God showed me the vision because He wanted to set me up to have *vision* of *His provision* to bring to pass what He *promised* me. He caused me to focus my spiritual binoculars to see clearer than ever before. You see, I tried to erase the words and statements that I'd written in my typewritten journal months after I'd written them, but as I started to put my computer's cursor at the point that the statements began, my computer shut down. Then I heard a voice telling me, "The vision *speaks*! Not in your time, but by *My Spirit*, where *time* doesn't exist, but *timing* is everything!"

"That's why the distractions have increased—because of timing. This is the time for manifestation and the completion of this story. Every time that you say no to all opposing voices in these final days of your test, and you obey *My voice* as I instruct you, you are moving in the direction of your destiny. Keep moving!" These were God's instructions to me.

During those final days of my test, I was pushed to the limits in order for the oil of God's anointing to flow properly to produce the Lauraine White that God originally intended me to be. You see, the enemy's assignment was to make me *fall* from grace. He wanted me to file for divorce. He wanted me to start dating other men that were pursuing me daily, all in direct response to what I perceived as being Michael's new life without me.

What was I *chosen* for? I was chosen to suffer. I was chosen to be an example of sacrifice. I was chosen to be betrayed. I was chosen to be laughed at and made fun of. I was chosen to be ridiculed and mocked. In the face of hardships, afflictions, adversities, it was necessary to choose to do the right thing although the pressure would cause me to want to retaliate or try to get back at those causing my hardship.

Ultimately, I was chosen to go to the pit of hell. At the end of January 2015, at the end of my day, I came into my bedroom and dropped all of my things on the floor. As I dropped my bags, I could feel myself falling. I was literally falling apart. But at the point of falling, I felt as if there were hands on the side of my left calf and around my left shoulder, and it was as if someone just picked me up. And that same person has been my constant companion throughout this process.

God wouldn't let me fall or fail. Part of my assignment was to go into the depths of hell, but He wouldn't let me go it alone. He entered the fiery pit with me—not just to support me but to *carry me* through to the finish line.

In the process, there were many lessons that I had to learn. I had to learn that it's not all about me, but all of this was for my good. I had to learn how to shape my game face and take this one for the team. I had to learn what it really means to love the way that God does, understanding that His ways *really* are not our ways—all that about "love is patient," "love is kind," "long-suffering," and all that jazz. I realized that our children were watching *how* I responded to every detail of what appeared to be betrayal, and I had to respond in ways that I didn't think were possible for me. I had to learn what it means to be family—that even though Michael and I were separated, we were still connected when it came to our family and those we loved. I learned what it means to have your heart broken but to still give unconditionally— and this in the face of my opposers, who were just waiting for me to do the wrong thing so that they could say, "Aha, I knew that's who she really was all the time!" I had to learn to forgive my husband, the other woman, family members that I perceived turned their backs on me, and ultimately, I had to forgive *me*.

During those twelve years, I made a lot of mistakes. I let everything and everyone that was dear to me go in order to pursue this process. That meant that I lost people that I will never have the opportunity to get back because they passed from this life. I had to forgive myself because I was following this road that God had me on, and if I got off to see about them during their crisis, I would have missed my assignment and ultimately missed my purpose. It wasn't easy to forgive myself for this because some of these people were very dear to me (aunts and uncles), and I am sure that they felt my not being there during their illnesses and other crises. My heart hurts as I look back and reminisce, but I had to forge ahead, knowing that God's plan and purpose were greater than what I gave up.

A part of my calling is to forgive without hesitation, and that includes forgiving myself. Early in life, I had to process forgiveness—it had to make sense for me to forgive, and it took years to accomplish. But now, understanding the heart of God, it is necessary for me to forgive first and understand later.

The necessary lesson for me was not to expect more than a person can give—even if they don't know that they don't have more to give. If they are here today, I learned to savor those moments—to live as if I may never see them again. At that moment, my life became so much richer because I gave up *expectations*. The rules changed. In fact, there were only two rules—*love* and *forgive*.

8

I CHOOSE TO COMMIT: A REASON TO SING AGAIN

Commit your way to the LORD; trust in Him and He will do this: He will make your righteous reward shine like the dawn, your vindication like the noonday sun.

PSALM 37:5–6

So, why this message? And why now? Our world is in a state of emergency. Crime rates are at an all-time high—including rape and murder. Since 2008 in Chicago alone, there have been more people murdered than soldiers killed in Iraq. We are building more prisons than schools. And schools are no haven for our children—not just for teaching, but for the safety necessary to ensure an environment that is conducive to learning.

Even our weather patterns reflect that something is out of sync with nature—the tsunamis, hurricanes, and earthquakes where they've never been before, planes disappearing, hundreds of birds falling out of the sky, and multitudes of fish found dead, washed up on the shore for no apparent reason—all of these unusual occurrences. Why? There seems to be no way out...

Except that God's perfect plan is for the Church to accept the mission that she has been given—not just to hear the cry of the nation but to respond with thoughtful yet radical answers. Answers that can only be found in Jesus Christ!

The physically sick go to the hospital. The spiritually sick should come to the Church to receive deliverance from what ails them—both in the natural and in the spirit. But many have left the Church because they found no solutions to their problems, and many times they are worse off than they were before coming to the Church. The reason for this is that we have church leaders that are ill-equipped to meet the needs of their people because they are filling their coffers with the offerings instead of feeding the poor, healing the sick, giving spiritual direction to those that have lost their way, and offering prayers that God answers because of their consecrated lifestyles.

In essence, if the Church is the hospital and Jesus is the physician, it would be safe to say that church leaders would be classified as nurses or nurse practitioners. They are to prep the patient, check vital signs, etc. Then they reenter the room with the physician as he/she examines and treats the patient.

What we are experiencing today are spiritual nurses, or church leaders, that never learned how to check the patients' vital signs. They can't even see that there is a problem. They don't know what a stethoscope looks like, let alone how to use one. Their education only provided for memorization of the material, rote understanding of vocabulary, history lessons, and how to "wear the uniform." But no practical exercises to demonstrate that they are now qualified to function in their skill area.

It is this practical side to this spiritual hospital that has to exist in order for it to remain effective. How many hospitals do you know of that would remain in business if they did not make you feel better after a procedure or after taking provided medications? Not many. Yet, that is what is happening in churches all over this nation. People go to worship services one way and come out exactly the same—or worse off. When I say worse off, it is because of the demands and constraints placed on God's people by their leaders—constraints that even those same leaders can't follow properly themselves, but still they insist on putting added work or pressure on those following them. It's all to justify the hierarchy that they have established, so that these followers will have something to grasp for in their hungry pursuit of position. But their attempts are futile at best.

Don't mention the art of praying. Many prayer ministries that function under these churches fail to demonstrate God's power to move mountains because of a lack of anointing. The presence of the Holy Spirit directing the operation is what is missing. Frankly, much of this is because the ones appointed to lead the groups worked their way up by grasping for position instead of consecrating themselves on their knees in prayer, with evidence of their labor through answered prayers. They didn't think that it was *even possible* to move all of heaven and earth—even change the weather patterns—through their prayers.

So, we have seen prayer ministries pop up over the internet, through social media, or by conference calls because those most anointed to operate in these areas were looked over by church leaders or were threats to the leadership. Those leaders couldn't stop what God placed in these anointed vessels because He is the One who orchestrated these gifts to be used—not suffocated or snuffed out by insecure leaders.

Even our children, whom we raised to know and understand that Jesus is the *only* way to God, have turned away from the Church as their source of inspiration. Many of our children have chosen to follow the Muslim and Buddhist faiths in large part because of the results that they perceive come out of lives devoted to God outside of the Church. They want you to show them what you're working with.

As a result, idols have become commonplace because of the migration of Christians to the Muslim or Buddhist faiths. Out of ignorance, they purchase, bring into their homes, and/or wear around their necks idols that were produced by these religious sects as objects of worship. Their ignorance is our fault because we have failed to educate and demonstrate that God's Law teaches that we are to have no other gods before Him—and exactly *what* that means.

But the message of this book is that God is tired of being second to His creation. No more discussion about "if you tithe, you will be blessed." God's message today is, "Bring order and obedience back to My house—beginning with My priests, pastors, and preachers—then I will restore!" In this hour, God does not need our money. He wants our hearts devoted to Him and only Him.

Through this twelve-year process, God taught me many things. The main lesson learned is that God can and *will* shut down everything in order to get us to do exactly what He intends for us to do.

God did it to me. He began to pour these messages into me in 2006 and 2007. One of the first visions that I received was of a forest with really tall trees that, in an instant, burned to the ground. They were immediately consumed by fire, and in a matter of seconds, all that was left was smoke rising from the pile of ashes. I later learned that this vision was significant to this writing. There was one central theme to all of it: the trees represented leaders—specifically, church leaders—and the resulting ashes from the consuming fire were evidence of the demise of those leaders.

Over and over again, God would cause me to weep over an issue then write what I was hearing. But because I was so busy with a business and family, most of the time, I was preoccupied by other things. Which brings me to my point—God had to shut everything down in order to get my attention, moving all obstacles out of the way.

I lost businesses. I lost relationships. Years went by (between 2007 to 2013) without a business, job, or other source of income—yet all of our bills got paid. We didn't lose anything. But I still didn't understand. I thought it was about me. God was blessing me, right?

When we could no longer afford to pay the mortgage, God caused Congress to pass laws to force mortgage companies to modify mortgages of the long-term unemployed. They even approved the giveaway of millions of dollars to homeowners that were out of work, just to help them make their mortgage payments. Congress also extended the unemployment benefits so that I received benefits for well over two years.

I couldn't see the forest for the trees. All of these events and occurrences were for one thing and one thing only—to give me the opportunity to tell this story. God took this country girl from Georgia and caused me to go through these sets of experiences so that He could deliver this message to His Church.

Out of *fear*, I would not initially obey God regarding the completion of this project. I wanted to rationalize with God that this was "just" a journal. I feared what religious men and women would think of me. I was concerned about how it would be received. Similarly to Jonah…

But remember, the fish swallowed Jonah because he tried to run away from God's assignment. Like Jonah, I almost got swallowed up by a set of circumstances that, if they had continued, would have cost me my life. Looking back, I can see God prodding and pushing me into my destiny, but I was reluctant. God showed me in the last three years that He could destroy me and/or my world as I knew it if I didn't obey Him—through sickness and losing those that I love; children losing their minds; husbands, without understanding why, having affairs; four years without any income.

Is it worth the compromise? I promise you, it is not! I went through years of hearing that we would have "an experience" with God. As I, through the prompting of the Holy Spirit, complete this writing, I am reminded that as a carrier of His presence, I didn't need to look for a temporary fix as a crack addict would. I learned to live in His presence, and living in His presence *required* my *obedience*.

Early Sunday morning on January 4, 2015 (as I completed this writing), God began to deposit a message of *change* in my spirit.

God woke me up with an assignment—to once again read Ezekiel 37, which is most commonly referred to as the chapter on the valley of the dry bones. See, I was so caught up in the flesh and what was happening to me that I couldn't see what God was trying to teach me and the world—that even though we forsake Him—just as my husband had done to me—all He wants to do is reconcile us to Himself.

The Scripture plainly states that there is now no condemnation, but our deeds must be judged. For, the Scriptures also state: "Shall we continue in sin that grace may abound?"[3] God forbid! It is God's love for us that makes Him suffer *long*. God taught me through years of suffering that when you truly love someone, you endure for love's sake alone.

---

3. Romans 6:1 NKJV.

This is God's dilemma as He has watched for centuries as His Church, originally set apart for His glory, moves away from the foundational things that caused God to favor her. The Lord Jesus built His Church on righteous ideals even though much wrong has been done since. God favors those that seek *after Him*.

God brought me to this point to make me intercede. He wanted me to feel the way He feels when we stray from Him. And boy, did I ever feel what He feels—only a fraction of what He feels, but I was literally shaking from confusion. The enemy surely had shot his best shot at me, and by all indications, he was winning the fight. But God said *no*! God asked me, "What do you want?" I didn't know what I wanted—I just knew that I was hurting and I wanted it to stop. God said, "Then speak to your circumstance. Tell your circumstance what it is going to be. It is whatever you say it is." God caused me to begin to decree that my marriage would last, just as He promised.

I got excited—all of a sudden I felt better. And all I did was speak to it— nothing had changed yet. In my excitement, I took this theory further. I began to decree that my family was blessed; my children were blessed; my yet-to-be-born grandchildren were blessed; our finances were blessed; my emotions were lining up with the Word of God; I was the *head* and not the tail; I was always *above* and never beneath. And I began to break the spirit of confusion that was over me and my husband—to break the spirit of perversion, lack, doubt, unbelief—but most importantly, I began to break the spirit that came to *destroy the promises of God*.

But as He caused me to decree and declare these things for my marriage, home, and family, God said that this is what He does for us through the Holy Spirit. The Word of God says that the Comforter makes intercession for us through groaning—even when we are unaware of it.

In between writing these things, I had an unusual amount of elimination—a lot more than normal. It appeared that all of my bad eating habits over the thirty days of holidays between Thanksgiving, Christmas, and New Year's that year were being eliminated in a single hour.

Then I became very tired—so much so that I needed to lie down again. When I started to lie down, I heard the Spirit say, "Look at the clock." It was ten a.m. The hour of worship services. I had already made the decision to stay at home from church that day, a Sunday, to complete this book because the Spirit of God told me that January 4 was my deadline to complete this work.

When I lay down, I fell asleep quickly. Then I felt my stomach cramping again, and I had to go back to the bathroom. As I was headed to the bathroom, I heard the Spirit of God say:

I AM causing an uncomfortable *elimination* in My Church. In the same way that you are *prophetically* eliminating this morning, I AM causing elimination to occur. I allowed you to become *fat* during these past twelve years, without being able to lose those unwanted pounds, as a representation of My Church. In Jewish culture, the number twelve is representative of *government*. I AM dealing with the *government* of My Church. My Church has become too *fat* and out of shape. That's because she will not *exercise*. She has become flabby because muscles are meant to be exercised. You can't lie around and eat and eat and eat without exercise, expecting to stay in shape.

The muscles of My Church are the spiritual gifts that I have given to them. You must *use them*. My Church is *weak* and *impotent* because of a lack of using what I have already given them. You have pastors and so-called spiritual leaders that *cannot* get a prayer through to Me, but they are considered *great preachers*. They *cannot* pray away disease. They *cannot* lay hands on the sick and they recover—these are basic exercises! Don't even mention *prophesying* over your government to see change happen, or *raising the dead*.

I *never* begin a *new chapter* without first closing the old one. The close of your 2014 closed the *book* on the reign of *terrorism* in

My Church. No longer will I *allow* leaders or lay people to destroy and disrupt *My flow.* Just as I turned over the money tables in the temple, I AM once again turning the tables over. Those that are called by My name will once again obey Me and do what I did, and not just because of a *gift* but because they authentically *walk with Me.*

Just as I AM making you over again, causing you to drastically lose weight within a short period of time, I AM doing the same with My Church. My Bride will be lean, with *everything* in the *right places.*

I AM coming to fix *everything.* Yes! It's *time* to renovate *My house.* I AM giving *every church* and its leaders *opportunity* to *restructure* and *reorder* so that I AM *the one and only head again.* If they do not comply, they will die, along with their kingdoms. I mean what I say, and I will do it! I AM God and Savior. Some think that because of grace I won't bring them to this end, but the *only* thing that will stop Me *now* is their changed hearts and lives.

It is time for My Church to wake up out of her slumber. Rise up and do that which I have called you to do. I AM a loving and gentle Savior, but I am also an angry and jealous God. You cannot do what you want to any longer and think that you can stay in My presence. It's your choice: *gifts* without *presence*, or *gifts* because of *presence.* Everything that's not like Me is coming down—mark My words, says the Spirit of the Lord.

Ezekiel 13:3 (KJV) tells us: "Woe unto the foolish prophets, that follow their own spirit, and have seen nothing!" Too many say all is well when calamity is at the door. They give false reports to strengthen those on the path to destruction. Let us beware of false prophets whose imagination is fired by lies to get gain from the poor and whose divinations are a lie. *Raise up men of God, Lord!*

I *never* begin a *new chapter* without first closing the old one. The close of your 2014 closed the *book* on the reign of *terrorism* in *My Church*.

God has prepared prophets in this hour who will stand—in the midst of ridicule and being ostracized—to bring correction and order. No other reason. Those with prophetic gifts that have pimped their gifts for fame and fortune give men what they want to hear, but a true prophet ordained by God brings correction, no matter what it costs. They cannot stand in the midst of chaos and not command the atmosphere to shift and align with God's order.

I can tell you—God prepared me to deliver this message. It was not by accident that these two bishops just happened to cross our paths. It was ordained and orchestrated by God Almighty. I used to sing a song, "Order My Steps," and little did I know that the words of that song would ring true in my life. God ordered my steps to witness and experience the sincere and authentic ministries of these men—spiritual giants in our lifetime and in their own right—only to reveal to us that even in our sincerity, we can miss God.

But there are foundational principles that we cannot miss. The first law is to love the Lord your God with all your heart and with all your soul and with all your strength and with all your mind. We cannot elevate anyone or anything above God. We must tear down every altar that we have erected, whether it be people, places, or things.

Then we must *repent*—turning from our wicked ways and turning to a place where we worship God *only*. I make this statement to stand out from everything else because it is the *single*, most essential element to us *changing* our world. We must be united in this change.

We, the Church, are standing at an important threshold—a very pivotal moment in time. We must choose this day whom we will serve—will we serve the God of all creation, or man? We cannot waiver in days ahead—we must secure our children's future and the inheritance of our nation. Whom will *you* serve?

9

I CHOOSE TO LOVE

Love is patient, love is kind. It does not envy, it does not boast, it is not proud. It does not dishonor others, it is not self-seeking, it is not easily angered, it keeps no record of wrongs. Love does not delight in evil but rejoices with the truth. It always protects, always trusts, always hopes, always perseveres.

1 CORINTHIANS 13:4–7

an love be found in suffering? The place of suffering provides the incubator for love to grow and develop. It's a place where, if left alone, love will wither and die. But if it is nurtured, love will, at the appointed time, blossom like a flower.

But can a flower blossom or bloom in a garden of concrete—where circumstances harden until they are like concrete and choke the life out of any potential that the planted seed has for growing and developing into what it was purposed to be?

Ah! Yes! That place where the concrete lies is *life*, and life has a way of snuffing all potential for love from a person. But God is there, sending situations and people that are used to break up the concrete ground in order that love can grow.

If you know anything about gardening, there are times when you must plant your seeds in a planter box and bring it inside to ensure that squirrels and other animals don't come along to eat the seeds out of the soil. You're hiding your crop so that it can grow and develop without outside forces tampering with its potential.

That is what God has to do—shelter us from those that will try to snatch us out of His hand. But there is a *place*...

> *Whoever dwells in the shelter of the Most High will rest in the shadow of the Almighty. I will say of the LORD, "He is my refuge and my fortress, my God, in whom I trust." (Psalm 91:1–2)*

That place—I never thought I would find the place where I could love again. It is a secret because most people will never find this place. What should have taken me out became a launching pad for me to begin again. Who would have ever thought that I would come out of this with my sanity and a resolve to do what I was born to do?

This is a place where validation is no longer a requirement. After the death of my mother, I needed the comfort of my husband's love and appreciation, but it wasn't offered to me. I measured my worth based on his approval rating of me—this was a big mistake.

In his absence, I grieved for the living instead of the dead. When a person dies, you have a funeral. But when a marriage dies, there's divorce and separation. Therefore, the grieving seems to never end. There's no final act to the story, which causes the process to take so much longer to go through. But the process of refining me brought me to this place where I was no longer searching for his validation. God made it clear to me that He chose me, and that's all the validation that I needed.

This is a place where every moment has meaning that moves you forward toward manifestation of the *promise*. Many times, I felt that moving forward meant moving on, but God had another plan. God orchestrates all of the moments, and He makes the decision when it is time to move on.

Throughout this process, I saw myself as a victim, but I am not a victim anymore. God caused me to see my life in a different light where it is no longer about cause and effect but about purpose. Everything that I endured caused me to prepare for my purpose. It was all divinely ordered. Without the pain, the purpose would not have had the power that is being realized even now.

This is a place where I learned how to communicate with God. Some would say that prayer is one-sided—that you should pray and meditate because prayer is the part that we play in communicating with God, and meditation is God's answer that we wait for. This suggests that we are the initiators of both—not God. But I submit to you that we should revisit prayer as God intended. Prayer includes meditation and is initiated by God—not us. Just as a husband and wife become one during sexual intercourse, where each gives and receives ways of expressing their love for the other through this mode of communicating with each other, so is prayer with God. It is a give-and-take process. Just as sexual intercourse—this single act—is vital to the marriage relationship and changes with time and age, so our prayer life with God is vital and changes. As the relationship develops, the process of prayer sweetens.

While in prayer long before I entered this twelve-year period of time, I found myself asking God for a *breakthrough*. What I didn't realize then was asking for a breakthrough *causes* a breakdown first. And who wants to go through the process of breaking? But the breaking causes the new to be birthed.

It is a new birth where I have the audacity to not only live again but to love again. Whom am I loving? Of course, my life in Jesus, the Christ, has grown to a pinnacle that I didn't even think existed, but I also found a "me" that I didn't think was possible to love. Getting here hasn't been easy. I can't say that I am unbroken because the breaking process is what brought me to this place.

How do you find the place in the midst of chaos? Can you *really* find refuge when everything in your world that means anything to you comes crashing down on you?

After September 11, 2001, we spoke of "ground zero," and after that began a season of redevelopment and recapturing the essence of who we are as Americans. It also began a period when we as a nation had to assert our military strength to prove to the world that we would not take what was done to us lying down.

September 11, 2002 began a twelve-year period of spiritual warfare for me when I found myself a slave to religion. I was in a prison of sorts—not one that others placed me in but one where I locked myself in my own chains. I closed the iron bars on myself, all in a ritualistic attempt to find God—a God that says that He came that we may have life. Instead of choosing the freedom that He offered, I confused the process and accepted a personal prison sentence. This journey of enslavement brought me to this place where I learned how to hear and obey God instead of man—where I learned the art of spiritual warfare. I learned how to fast and pray—how to "shut in" in order to hear from God. How to mark His voice so that I would not follow another.

> I was in a prison of sorts—not one that others placed me
> in but one where I locked myself in my own chains.

There were periods of time during this twelve-year ordeal when I fasted more than I ate because I was developing my relationship with God in such a way that I thought that my works would get God's attention. You know— it was my interpretation of "faith without *works* is *dead*," right?

At the end of this twelve-year period of time, I saw my life appear to unravel, with the closing of our businesses, my son battling PTSD, short selling our home, the folding of our pastorate, moving in with my mother until we purchased a new home, my mother's illness and eventual death, then my husband's infidelity, and finally him moving out of our home. All of this was meant to break me. But breaking me was the very thing that I needed to prepare me fully for my calling.

You see, I was confusing my decisions based on events that had occurred. With each occurrence mentioned above, God helped me move beyond the immediate to the next step. But in all of the chaos of that last year, I got caught up in the act of my husband's infidelity. I couldn't seem to move beyond the facts. I wanted to dwell on what he did, and so did the enemy of my soul. The enemy knew that if he could keep me in the place where I was consumed with what Michael was doing, I would miss my assignment and the new place God had for me. That was the goal. He knew that if he could keep me from the new place, that I would miss the power and the new and fresh anointing.

This marked the breaking—breaking my will in order to get to God's will. God caused me to see that all that was happening was smoke and mirrors to keep me from focusing on the big picture. My husband wasn't my enemy, and neither was the other woman. My enemy was Satan, and he doesn't fight fair. He's cunning and undermining. He hits below the belt and doesn't care whom he takes out in order to accomplish what he intends. We are just pawns to him.

From the beginning, Satan has been angry with us because God said He made us in His image and likeness, which was what Satan wanted more than anything—to be like God. Therefore, he and his army of angels work tirelessly to keep us from believing in our worth to God.

But God taught me to look beyond the immediate to see what's ahead. This wasn't possible without the breaking. Many days, I thought I would lose my mind, but it was all necessary so that I lined up with God's process of refinement.

I was a control freak for way too long, and God can't use anyone that has to do things their way. I spent too many years controlling people and things. I wanted things done my way because that was the *only* right way, right? There is something to be said for willpower, but it has no place with the things of God. Willpower, or imposing our will on others, really is self-power, and at some point, it fails us. In Romans 8:28–39, Paul deals with one idea: being called means conforming to the image of Jesus Christ for the sheer sake of the call.

And we know that in all things God works for the good of those who love Him, who have been called according to His purpose. For those

God foreknew He also predestined to be conformed to the image of His Son, that He might be the firstborn among many brothers and sisters. And those He predestined, He also called; those He called, He also justified; those He justified, He also glorified. What, then, shall we say in response to these things? If God is for us, who can be against us? He who did not spare His own Son, but gave Him up for us all—how will He not also, along with Him, graciously give us all things? Who will bring any charge against those whom God has chosen? It is God who justifies. Who then is the one who condemns? No one. Christ Jesus who died—more than that, who was raised to life—is at the right hand of God and is also interceding for us. Who shall separate us from the love of Christ? Shall trouble or hardship or persecution or famine or nakedness or danger or sword? As it is written: "For Your sake we face death all day long; we are considered as sheep to be slaughtered." No, in all these things we are more than conquerors through Him who loved us. For I am convinced that neither death nor life, neither angels nor demons, neither the present nor the future, nor any powers, neither height nor depth, nor anything else in all creation, will be able to separate us from the love of God that is in Christ Jesus our Lord.

But enduring the hardships and the pain of this twelve-year journey left me broken, downtrodden, and crawling across the floor in an attempt to stay alive. I was fighting for my destiny.

I was raw and empty inside. God had to peel back the layers of my pain in order for me to deal with the past so that I could move ahead to my future.

In dealing with my past, I had to make peace with the demons that I had allowed to cloud my ability to love. I lived almost twenty-one years with my husband's mother, and I treated her as an outsider. I had to be raw and real with myself and acknowledge the part that I played in the breakdown of our relationship. Yes, we both played a part in the mess that we made, but I worked to perpetuate the demise of any potential that we had to not just get along but develop a real loving relationship with each other.

When I asked my mother-in-law to move in with us after the diagnosis of cancer that she received, many people told me that it would be impossible for two women to live under one roof. At the time, all I knew was that she needed our support during this fight for her life, and I was not going to turn my back on her just because the odds were against us being able to live together.

Almost from the beginning, there appeared to be a silent power struggle between us—struggle in who would care for the children, who would cook, or in demeaning me because I didn't make cooking a priority. All of this put the relationship that had once been a friendship into a pressure cooker, and you know what happens when things are put under pressure. They end up exploding.

Therefore, for years, we appeared to tolerate rather than care for each other—all for the sake of my husband and our children. This was a big mistake. What a treasure I was missing!

Hindsight can be 20/20. Looking back over my life, specifically the last twenty-one years, I realized that I never looked at my mother-in-law as a woman with flaws. I saw her as my husband's mother—the mother hen that I perceived her to be. I never looked at her for who she was as a woman that had lived her life, raised her son as a single parent, and sacrificed to pay for private school for him—a woman who loved and was loved, who had been hurt tremendously yet lived out loud and on purpose.

What opened my eyes to this realization was my mother. Right before she transitioned from this life, she helped me to see my mistake in overlooking my mother-in-law's strengths. She helped me to see the value in her life's story.

Prior to my mother receiving the diagnosis of pancreatic cancer, my mother-in-law lived with her. Once the diagnosis came, my mother's outlook on life changed, and her overall health diminished almost overnight. We were then thrust into survival mode. We had to devise a plan to care for her and seek out immediate solutions for her health conditions. Everywhere that we went, it appeared that no one gave my mother much hope for survival. Every doctor that we went to only offered pain management and palliative care.

The survival mode that we went into wasn't just for our mother—it was for us too. How do we go on without Mama? We *needed* her to survive— or so it seemed. Almost daily, I travelled forty miles one-way to my mother's home to see after her needs, but it was my mother-in-law that dug in to care for my mother most of the time. It was my mother-in-law that made sure that my mother took her medicine and supplements three times a day, that she got a bath every day, and that she got dressed and out of bed for several hours a day.

I spent most of my time cleaning and making sure that the house was in a presentable order because I knew my mother loved a clean house and didn't like for guests to come over when the house was a mess. Each time, my mother would urge me to leave the housecleaning and come sit down to talk to her. It was almost as if she knew her time wasn't long, and she had some final things to impart to me. Although reluctant, I began to do as she asked and found treasure in those moments. After becoming an adult, my relationship with my mother developed such that she became more of a mentor than a mother. She shared with me how proud she was of me, but she saw some things that I needed to do better. My mother always saw the good in people, and she colored her words in such a way that it would always turn out positive, even when she was scolding you. She encouraged me to spend more time loving and caring for my husband, and she wanted me to take a second look at my relationship with my mother-in-law.

My mother took me down memory lane. She pointed out times when I had neglected and many times was downright ungrateful for things that my mother-in-law had gone out of her way to do for our children. She helped me to see that the times when I had problems with my husband, I took it out on my mother-in-law.

But how do you fix the wrongs of your past? After so many years of bad behavior, how could I make it right?

After this encounter with my mother, I had it in my heart to celebrate my mother-in-law's seventieth birthday by hosting a party with all of her friends. I found out that my mother-in-law had never really had a birthday party in her life, and I felt that was a way that I could show my love and gratitude for her.

Soon after this encounter, my mother transitioned, but I was grateful that she gave me direction in this area of my life. Her motto was to let love be your guide, and if I was to live my life differently, I, too, would love deliberately, always seeking the best for the other person and not selfishly looking out only for myself.

There's a higher calling that I had to arise to accept, and that was to find the best, grab hold of it, and give it away to those that I love. And my love is now extended beyond those in my immediate family. It extends to the universal family.

Yes…Love…This four-letter word is powerful. But what's love got to do with anything? It is the main ingredient necessary to revive us as individuals as well as the Church and eradicate any and everything that is exalted above God.

It was love that caused me to go through a twelve-year wilderness experience in order for God to reveal His concern for His Church. It was love that caused me to remain in a marriage where acts of infidelity compromised the sanctity of it.

It is God's love that has been long-suffering in watching as we have displayed our detestable idols before Him in His own house. It was God's love that orchestrated all of these events and put me on the course that ultimately changed the destiny of my entire family. What's love got to do with it? Everything!

Some would say that love isn't enough to revive a marriage that has failed. I found out through my own life experiences that it starts and ends with love. It's love that causes a man torn between two women to make a choice, and it's not always the obvious—to choose between what is understood and comfortable and what is new and fresh.

Is it possible for that which is old, understood, and comfortable to become new and fresh again? That's exactly what God had planned for our marriage. God promised months before that He would make our relationship new and fresh—reviving it from the dead. Never underestimate the power of God's Word spoken over your life.

Idol worship, as I learned through the parallel with my life, is very similar to the act of infidelity. There is broken intimacy. And we have become too comfortable with both.

You can't fix what you don't know is broken. Just as we have become desensitized to the effects of defiling the marital bed, we see no wrong in elevating a man to the point of making him equal with God. This rips apart our relationship with God—we are choosing to *love* both, and how can we? We say we love "the God" in the man, but have we taken it much farther than that?

As the Scripture so eloquently states, "No man can serve two masters." God's original intent for our relationship with Him and in marriages is to have a singular devotion. Without this devotion or celebration, the love fades. That's what happened in our marriage. I took my husband for granted. I neglected him, and he neglected me. And when I had opportunity to celebrate him, I put others and other things ahead of him.

Yeah, he was the one that stepped out on our marriage—more than I care to acknowledge—but I stepped out long before he ever did. I missed taking care of his needs and making him king of his castle. Our children didn't celebrate him as king because I didn't—I didn't know how important that was until he left. Then it was as if someone ripped my heart out. I realized the error of my ways too late in the game.

Earlier, Michael pursued no relationships—just going to strip clubs and fly-by-night flings. But fast forward twelve years, and instead of a fling, he pursued a relationship with someone who had the potential of replacing me as his wife. She said all the right things that pushed his buttons. They even prayed together ("There is a way that seems right…"). Although they had no connection with God because of their choices, they could pervert God's interpretation of their actions by saying, "God will forgive us!"

This reminds me of the Scripture in Romans 6:1–2 (KJV), where Paul asks, "Shall we continue in sin, that grace may abound? God forbid!"

Michael came to a crossroads and had to make a decision—Do I choose my wife or the other woman whom I desire to be with?

In essence, he made the other woman his idol—the one that replaces the original. The problem with idols is that they will never produce the end result that he expects them to—the happiness that he presumes that he needs. Only One can fulfill that desire, and that is God.

The biggest lie that Satan perpetuates is that we should be in pursuit of happiness. God never promised us happiness. He wants us to pursue joy, which transcends happiness. Happiness is temporary, but joy is eternal.

What Michael didn't realize was that I, too, was at a crossroads. For the first time in my life, I had the *power*—power to not just acknowledge but command my life to be what I wanted it to be. I knew what I wanted and what I didn't want, and I was not going to accept substitutes, counterfeits, or less than what I deserved. I deserved a husband that was faithful to me—not having a roaming eye, seeking other lovers.

Twelve years ago, Michael would not leave me or our home—he insisted on working out our differences. Now, he could leave. What would cause him to bail out on our marriage of twenty-one years? It was desperation—an uneasiness because he couldn't juggle keeping both relationships going successfully, although he wanted to.

This same desperation is prevalent in the Church today. Many have left the Church because they have become disenfranchised by the "giving" frenzy that takes place every Sunday morning. How many times do you really need to pass the offering plate in order to pay the bills of the church? Too much debt has caused church leaders to snuff the life out of its members in order to keep up appearances.

Many people, those that God loves, have left the Church because they feel worthless. With all the pursuit of titles, many have grown cold toward weekly church attendance because in all of their pursuits, they are still empty inside. I have watched as faithful members give…and give…and give. Not just of their money but also their valuable time. And no one cares. Or so it seems.

Then there are the church leaders that hit on the female (and male) members. They abuse privileges that they shouldn't be given. Some have gone as far as to tell these women and men that God told them to have sex with them, or that they had a dream of them having sex and therefore, God must want them to do so. Abuse of this power defaces God's love, which is honest, true, and always seeks our highest and best good.

How do we fix this? Will putting away idol worship eradicate these problems? No, but it's a start.

Becoming fulfilled through our worship has to be secondary. First, we must prioritize the fix. We cannot be consumed with validation for what we do; we must act because it is the right thing to do.

God's design has to be our number-one priority. But how do we move forward? Second Chronicles 7:14 states, "If My people, who are called by My name, will humble themselves and pray and seek My face and turn from their wicked ways, then I will hear from heaven, and I will forgive their sin and will heal their land."

There must be a change—a change in focus—a change in where we put our energies. This change will cause us to surrender our will to God's, understanding that in surrendering we gain position and purpose to move beyond the "me" mentality to the "we." Collectively, we move God. And when we are united in our purpose of tearing down our idols, God moves heaven and earth for us.

But is the message that I am purporting that I am one of only a few chosen ones? No, far from it! I believe that we are all chosen in this hour to be the change that needs to occur in the Lord's Church, but we must *choose* God in return. Remember, we are a generation chosen to change the world. God doesn't need many to make the change, but each of us plays a role—no matter how small or large—and each is valuable to the transformation.

Then what's behind this whole notion that we are chosen? Chosen for what? There are so many benefits that we have as God's chosen, but most of us never exercise or use these benefits. These benefits are for the entire body to move us into this area of *change*.

The Word of God speaks of the nine gifts of the Spirit, which are listed in Scripture in 1 Corinthians 12, and they are:

1. Word of wisdom

2. Word of knowledge

3. Faith

4. Gifts of healing

5. Working of miracles

6. Prophecy

7. Discerning of spirits

8. Divers kinds of tongues

9. Interpretation of tongues

So, just as my husband and I have the choice to love each other again, we, the Church, have a choice to make. Will we choose to live for, love, and obey God? Will we become that city on a hill that's not afraid to shine the light, understanding that *light* belongs in darkness and therefore banishes it? Or will we continue down the path that is destroying our world one family at a time through disastrous circumstances? Will we die in this place? I choose to *love* and run into my destiny, which encompasses the good, the bad, and the ugly.

I choose to tear down all *altars* that I erected to people, places, and/or things. I made a declaration that as for *me* and *my house*, we will *serve* the *Almighty and Living God*! And Him *only* will we serve!

10

LOVE WINS

When I was a child, I loved playing the game hide and seek. In case you don't know the basis of the game, there's one person who is the seeker, and everyone else hides. The person chosen to seek covers their eyes, turns to a wall or object, and counts down from a predetermined number while everyone else looks for a place to hide where they're not easily discovered. Ten, nine, eight, seven…

When the seeker finishes counting down, they finish by saying "Ready or not, here I come," and the seeker goes on a hunt for those hiding. When the seeker uncovers someone in their hiding place, the seeker screams out, "Tag, you're it."

If the seeker doesn't find anyone in their hiding place, the seeker shouts out, "Come out, come out, wherever you are."

It's been seven years since I first published this book, and since then I have found myself playing the hide-and-seek game of life. I've been seeking the real reasons for my assignment. I looked for clues everywhere, trying to find the hidden messages behind the closed and open doors I've encountered.

The essence of the story is that the real reasons for the attacks and the answers that I was seeking were all hidden in plain sight. All through the process, the Spirit of God kept telling me that all the things that came against me and my household were just *smoke and mirrors*. They were not real. They were only distractions sent to conceal the real answers I was seeking.

The ultimate question for me was, Why would God want me to take back an unfaithful, disrespectful, and ungrateful man when he came asking for forgiveness and to take him back the moment he came back? The idea, from the day the Spirit gave utterance to me until the weekend before I wrote this chapter in October 2023, made me sick to my stomach. Even in the sick feeling, though, I answered God's request with a yes. What else could I do? God has been too good to me. I told Him that I would obey Him, but it was a half-hearted yes.

I wasn't all in. I was afraid of what I would look like to everyone. I would look like the dumbest person ever. I felt as if I would be considered by him and everyone else to be a doormat—the one used in the middle of winter to trample on and remove the dirt and grime under their feet. It seemed like a show of weakness, and I didn't want to be seen as weak. That's the last way I wanted to be perceived.

There are some things that God does that won't ever make sense—at least not until time reveals the essence of God's *why*. Like with Abraham—God told Abraham to take his son Isaac and sacrifice him. This was the same God that promised to give him a son, and now he was telling him to kill him.

It doesn't make sense. You don't read in Scripture whether or not this was something that Abraham had to wrestle with in his mind before moving toward this assignment. Did he immediately do this, or did it take some time for him to process everything before achieving this level of obedience? This was not an everyday type of assignment and definitely not what God will ask of everyone. So why did God ask this of Abraham over anyone else? Why would He make a promise and then appear to change His mind? Then, for Abraham to trust God enough to follow through on it, what was going through his mind?

Can you see Abraham explaining that one to Sarah? There's no Scripture reference to Abraham having any conversation with her about it. The only thing we read about is Abraham having conversations with God.

Can you imagine Sarah's reaction if Abraham came home alone—without her beloved son, Isaac? Did Abraham toss this over in his mind as to what he would say to her when he returned home empty-handed? Maybe he rehearsed what to say as he was figuring this all out, or maybe not. Scripture never tells us anything other than that he obeyed God. But the twenty-five years it took from the time that God made the promise the first time until the birth of Isaac tell a story.

I can only imagine what my reaction would've been if my husband came home to tell me that God had told him to sacrifice my only son, and now he was dead. A woman scorned doesn't adequately describe the fury I would feel. My first reaction would probably not be Christlike, that's for sure. Either I would fall dead in that moment, or he would be dead—from the knife in my hand.

The other issue that I have is that God told the Hebrews to sacrifice animals, not people. Did Abraham ever question God on that? After all, this could have been seen as hypocritical behavior for God.

Did God have to ask Abraham more than once? The Scripture doesn't say. These details are left out of Scripture, and we are left with questions. The questions arise because of our own struggles with obedience. And I'm writing this because of my own questions for God.

I struggle with obedience. I wrestle with the *why* of my assignments. Why me? Why am I the sacrificial lamb in this circumstance? Why should I have to suffer like this? Why should I have to wait and watch—wait for Michael to return and watch them as they continue to torture me with their betrayal? Why?

I'm not the one who immediately obeyed. I'm not the one who heard God's voice telling me what to do and then got up the next morning setting out to do it, as Abraham did. No. I waited. I needed to process the idea. I wrestled with God. I tried to change God's mind about it. Certainly, He didn't mean that for me, right? There must be another way to accomplish this without having to sacrifice my dignity.

As I told those that I love what God had told me to do, they worked to convince me otherwise. "You have a right to move on with your life," is what many of them expressed out of their sense of defensiveness of me.

Some looked at me as though I'd lost my mind. They felt that the God they knew wouldn't ask anyone to do anything such as this in light of all the pain and anguish that I've endured already.

But I'm not the only one that's gone through heartbreak or trauma. I'm in very good company. The older I get, the *more* I understand this fact. Just when you think you've got it bad, look around you. Thousands are suffering much more than you.

But when you're going through something, it's all about you. You want other people who see you go through it to know that it's not fair what's happening to you. You want someone to do something in your defense.

You cry out for help, but many times help never comes—or so it seems. What you get is a lot of advice. Everyone can see what you can't see. It's just that they're looking from their perspective, and everyone's got one.

Drowning in self-pity, you end up avoiding public places and family outings because it's just too terrible to tolerate. You walk into the room, and everyone gets quiet. It's the look on their faces that causes your stomach to curl. You don't want their pity.

You want to hear them say, "You need to obey God." That statement never came to me. Even with my siblings, I could feel their blood boil. They love me and wanted better for me.

Now I can sympathize with Noah. While building the ark, I'm sure people ridiculed and mocked him. They thought he'd lost his mind. He's crazy.

Rain? Enough rain that you'll need this size boat? Surely, he wanted to give up. I'm sure his family tried to convince him to stop with all this nonsense about a flood.

Oh, and we all know the story of Job and his so-called well-meaning friends. You remember. They came over to his house and, after seeing his condition, sat with him for seven days and seven nights without saying one word.

But when they started to talk, the essence of why they were there surfaced. I'm sure they thought highly of Job before all of this happened, but this was their aha moment. These rippling events that happened to Job reinforced their belief that maybe he wasn't as holy as he claimed.

He was all talk, they thought. Certainly, anyone who lived uprightly shouldn't have to go through anything like that. They gave him back the words that he'd used to encourage them.

You reap what you sow. They felt that Job must've done something to cause all these calamities to fall on him with such force. That's probably what some of my friends felt about me. Somewhere, somehow, I did something in my lifetime to deserve what I've lived through. There were times in the process that I, too, while wallowing in my circumstances, felt that I was somehow responsible.

Every time I said yes, a roadblock would appear. I would see or hear something about my husband that would make me go back to my see-saw answer—up and down—one day up but the next one down. It's called a yo-yo effect, and it's determined by external stimuli.

The yes that God was seeking from me had to be from the internal decisions that I made. The yes that would end this ball-and-chain experience had to be an unwavering, unshakable decision that was firmly grounded in something or someone greater than myself.

It's the waiting, though. I got caught up in having to wait. Okay, now that I've decided to obey, Lord, can't You just hurry up and get this thing over and done with? At the rate at which God was completing this, I kept changing my mind. I kept going back and forth—I'm going to do it, then I can't.

This was a puzzle that I couldn't seem to put together because the picture just kept getting blurrier and blurrier. The blurred lines weren't God's doing but mine. My emotions got in the way of my vision.

It became an emotional roller-coaster ride. I wanted to date again, but God wouldn't let me move past the first date with anyone. I had the Sarah syndrome. I had to help God out. He said that He was restoring me, but maybe

He meant with a new husband—not that old unfaithful one that stuck a knife in my back, turning it as he kept moving ahead. He couldn't mean that one.

He didn't change His mind about it even with all my pleading for a *ram-in-the-bush* experience. You know what I mean. I was hoping that God started with one sacrifice in mind to see if I really loved Him, and then once I proved that I did by *saying* that I did, He would go ahead and point me in the direction of my other options—ultimately the real sacrifice.

No, there was no ram in the bush. There were no other options but to do what He said. He was nice about it though. The Spirit of God gently reminded me that His message was consistently the same. He kept telling me that the things that I was seeing happen were just *smoke and mirrors*, but I didn't understand.

Just as Jesus did with the death of Lazarus—when Jesus heard that Lazarus was sick, he stayed where he was for another two days and boldly proclaimed that his sickness would not end in death. He just told the disciples that Lazarus had fallen asleep. When they got to Lazarus, the first news was that he was dead. Just like my marriage. Dead.

In the seven years since first publishing this book, Michael has tried to come back a few times, but most of the time, I gave a strong no because I knew the process wasn't finished. But after COVID-19 struck its blow, he became stricken with it, and because his best friend asked me to reach out to him, I did. I don't know if it was due to the crisis happening and his awareness of the brevity of life, but he asked me to give him another chance, and I did.

By this time, I'd moved to Richmond, Virginia, and we began dating long-distance. A lot of things for both of us had changed. We were not the same people. But because of the distance, I couldn't clearly see everything that I needed to see to understand whether or not it was the right time to move forward.

Unfortunately, it wasn't the right time. I realized that the Spirit of God had done an incredible amount of internal work within me that was unshakable. I came to visit him for his birthday, and I asked him a lot of questions that he didn't have answers to, and I realized that I didn't intend to go back to the same life that we had before. A part of that internal work was to see my value and not accept any less than what God had promised.

If it's not what you want, you've got to be strong enough to walk away from it. So, I did. The only regret that I have is that I didn't fully communicate to him why I walked away. I just stopped accepting his calls. I let them go to voicemail. I knew it had to be a hard stop for him to get the message.

He didn't know what God promised me. He just thought I would take him back and continue to put up with his mess. That's not what God promised me, and I wouldn't settle for anything less. The Spirit of the Lord promised that Michael's return would mirror what He is doing with His Church. He is causing His Church to return to its first love with faithfulness—not idol worship. So, if I allowed him to continue to be who he'd always been, I would be settling, and I didn't have time for that. God had work for me to do, and I couldn't be distracted with that kind of foolishness anymore.

But what about the promise? God's promise to me has not changed. He's still going to do what He promised me that He would do.

I had to see what was behind the smoke and mirrors. What was the reason for all the distractions? As life unfolded, it became crystal clear what the *why* was all about. It was my assignment to write and not just to write about anything but to write about what I've had the privilege to learn over the last twenty-one years.

I had to write about how I overcame and the process involved in getting me out of hell-bound circumstances. This was eye-opening. It changed my motivation. This revelation came through nine years of wrestling and wrangling to see what all the commotion was about. Peeling back the events that occurred over the years, brought to light in this exposure, gave me the courage to do what I was assigned to do. Writing about how hell came against my home and how God's rescue plan revived me was now unstoppable. Even with all the furious attacks against me, nothing could keep me from it. That's because I understood *why*.

This revelation occurred between July 13 and July 16, 2023, which was exactly nine years to the date that God gave the vision and promise of opening my Red Sea. It gripped my soul to parallel the moments with the knowledge that our Lord is always consistent and faithful.

It was during those four days that I pulled out the writing of my two books *The Way Out* and *Bulletproof* to revisit finishing them. It sealed my fate. As I read back through what I had written and what they covered, it became clear the reason why Satan pulled the big guns out on me.

These books teach lessons on spiritual warfare. Satan wants believers in Jesus to remain powerless. He wants us to stay sick and not take up the keys to the kingdom that Jesus left for us. He wants us to be afraid of receiving the Holy Spirit so that he can keep control of us and the order of things in the earth realm. He doesn't want to give up his control.

The keys are in our hands. Jesus finished everything
when He was nailed to the cross, and it was sealed
for eternity when He got up out of the grave.

It's for this very reason that the Son of God was made manifest, so that He destroys all works of the enemy, but we will never realize it if we don't exercise the dominion that's been given to us. The keys are in our hands. Jesus finished everything when He was nailed to the cross, and it was sealed for eternity when He got up out of the grave. But the exercise of this level of authority lies with us taking the keys and using them.

On October 7, 2023, which was the day of Simchat Torah and the end of the Feast of Booths or Sukkot, I received an alarming call from my daughter, who was hysterical on the other end of the call because on her way home from work, she'd had an accident. It was very serious. She was driving in the fast lane and hit a wall. My heart skipped a beat and almost exploded.

After the initial shock, I became very calm but assertive, trying to get more information out of her. She was so hysterical because after I gave her the car in June of this year, she didn't get insurance coverage. Therefore, she wouldn't be able to afford to repair the damages to the car.

I helped her to calm down and think through everything. She and I both had to stop and acknowledge our gratitude that she was still alive and okay. I know God protected her. Hallelujah! Right before she called, I had been wrestling with whether or not I would go to help with the food distribution at our church. All night Friday night, I'd turned the thought over in my mind, but the Spirit woke me up and told me not to go. Little did I know what was going to happen, but God did.

Before buying the Mustang for her in 2019, the Spirit of the Lord moved on me to buy a car for her. We never had a close relationship. She was always closer to her dad. But since our separation and divorce, she and I began to work to establish a better relationship. This idea to buy a car for her was to help in that effort. She's always been a very good child and a great student and never caused us one moment of heartache, so why not reward her?

When the Spirit of God told me to buy a Mustang, I was worried about her safety in such a fast car, but the Spirit reassured me that I needed to extend this olive branch to her. He told me that I would understand later.

In 2020, during COVID-19, my youngest two children moved to Puerto Rico, and I was left with their cars. I told them that we needed to settle the issue so that I was not left with three cars while living in a rental in Richmond, Virginia. Because of the resale values of my car and my youngest son's car, I ended up keeping the Mustang.

Fast forward three years, and they both moved back to the States—my daughter to Missouri and my son back to Atlanta. She wanted her car back, but I didn't have any transportation, and the prices of cars had escalated due to supply-chain issues. Therefore, I refused to give her the car until prices moderated.

Before returning to Atlanta, my son had an accident in the Mustang, but I didn't want my car insurance to go up, so I didn't file a claim to repair it. I found someone who could repair the minor damage done to the front bumper and paid for it out of pocket.

I didn't end up getting the repairs done until just before I was ready to buy a new car. Then I paid for my daughter to fly to Atlanta to pick up the car after I bought my new one. She was so excited, and I was excited for her.

Her move to Puerto Rico didn't just put her a great distance away in miles, but it put a great distance in our relationship with each other. Our relationship became almost nonexistent. She would only call me when she needed something. She didn't want to hear about God or religion—as if that were all we had to talk about. The devil thought he had her in his grip such that she would turn on me.

She put distance between us because she couldn't handle the idea of a conversation with me about God. She found me to be toxic, frigid, and stuck in my ways. Her thoughts were inundated with her need to find her own identity separate and apart from family. The enemy put depressing thoughts in her mind and wanted to send her into dark places. But God knew what the enemy meant for evil, and He had a plan to turn that evil around for our good and for His glory.

So, it seemed that the only connection she and I had at that point was the Mustang. But after the accident, she couldn't fathom that I would not be upset about the wrecked car without her having insurance to cover the damage or at least having funds to replace it. That's why she was so frantic on the call. She felt that she had failed me, and that knowledge moved her to tears.

My response blew her away—it wasn't expected. She knew in her heart that the worst part of the incident would be how I reacted to hearing that she didn't have insurance. But the most important thing to me was her safety. Knowing that she was alive and had not endured any injuries was the most important thing to me. I was grateful, and I let it be known to her. Coming into that understanding changed the trajectory of our relationship. She now saw me as a loving mother and not a scolding or toxic tyrant.

She hit a brick wall in the accident and in her life. It was a defining moment for her. After graduating from college, she struggled to find the place where she belonged. She was a caregiver to family members because that's her nature, but when a few died, she lost her way. She questioned many of the things that she was taught as a child, but hitting that wall changed the course of her life.

She came out of that accident looking at life through a new lens where hope abounds. And it was through the eyes of love that she came to the knowledge and understanding that she is accepted for who she is without hesitation. It's in that place that doors began to open up for her.

I believe it's the same with all of us. We hit the brick wall, and it causes us to pivot. The brick wall looks like a dead end, but it's really a doorway out of harmful and dreadful circumstances. It's at that point that we realize how much we need a loving Savior. It's a place where obedience is no longer a struggle. You want to follow the path set for you. That's the common thread between us—deciding to obey.

Can my obedience now still count for righteousness as Abraham's did? I believe so because Jesus said that the day we accept His invitation, He forgives and makes us righteous. That's a promise we can hold on to and cherish. His love just won't quit. He won't let go. He never throws in the towel. Love hopes for and bears all things. Love never fails.

ABOUT THE AUTHOR

Moments before taking the stage, Lauraine White appears to be a quiet and unassuming woman who is patiently standing on the outside of the spotlight. But as soon as she takes the stage and opens her mouth, her prophetic voice and soulfully melodic sound transcend time and prepare her listeners for worship with her unparalleled love songs devoted to Jesus Christ.

From a place of radical worship, God called Lauraine out of the business and religious world to be a prophetic voice in this season to this generation of seekers. This new season requires God's direction that only comes from HIS prophets. God uses Lauraine's musical abilities to open heavenly portals for those listening to experience new levels in worship, where God shows up and speaks through her. It is a worship experience like no other—God comes into the building, and His glory rests among those engulfed in the "behind-the-veil" experience. Angels' wings are left as evidence of their presence…gold dust is gently dusted on chairs and on the floor as evidence that divine visitations have taken place. Once you go there, it's hard to leave…

How did Lauraine come to be able to usher in such an experience? Through trials by fire! Every test—every trial—brought Lauraine to her knees in prayer, teaching her the art of warfare. God uses Lauraine's musical talents and piercing voice to penetrate the enemies' camps. After this time of testing, God positioned Lauraine to be formally trained and ordained by Apostle Wayne and Dr. Beverly Jackson and by the late Apostle Milton Perry.

Lauraine grew up attending the Church of Christ, where there was no instrumental music and where women did not play any role in ministry! But God, in His infinite wisdom, ordered Lauraine's steps, drawing her closer to HIM so that she understands that God created all instruments for His pleasure and that He can use a woman to minister to His people.

It was definitely God's plan to prepare Lauraine through her unique experiences as an entrepreneur, running a successful mortgage company; as a
battered wife—one who faced death three times at the hand of her first
husband; as one who faced poverty and being ostracized and rejected by
those that she thought loved her the most—in order to deliver an extraordinary message: that God wants to be reconciled to His children.

The question is why now and so late in her life? When God calls you, it
is on HIS time, not yours! It took forty years for Moses to receive his
commission to lead the children of Israel out of Egypt. It took seventeen
years of preparation before Joseph was delivered from slavery and imprison-
onment. It took twenty years before Jacob was released from Laban's control. Abraham and Sarah were in their old age when they finally received
their promise, Isaac. Lauraine White, at sixty-something, is uniquely positioned to carry this message because nothing else matters.

But Lauraine asks you this question: Is there anything too hard for God?